Book One in the "Christians in Business" Series

CHRISTIAN

Entrepreneur

How to Profit from your Ideas

DBN PUBlications

authorHOUSE

AuthorHouse™
1663 Liberty Drive
Bloomington, IN 47403
www.authorhouse.com
Phone: 833-262-8899

Published by AuthorHouse 05/28/2024

ISBN: 979-8-8230-2680-2 (sc)
ISBN: 979-8-8230-2679-6 (e)

Library of Congress Control Number: 2024910047

Print information available on the last page.

Table of Contents

Section I   **Creative Ideas Can Change Your World!**

Chapter 1   In the Beginning... 2
Chapter 2   Valuable Opportunities 12
Chapter 3   Benefits of Developing Your Ideas 18
Chapter 4   Let's Go Out There and Do Something........25

Section II   **Intellectual Property**

Chapter 5   Patents.. 30
Chapter 6   Trademarks 43
Chapter 7   Copyrights 50
Chapter 8   Trade Secrets 62
Chapter 9   Family Recipes 68
Chapter 10 Domain (Web Site) Names 72

Section III   **The Nuts and Bolts of Running a Business**

Chapter 11 Forming Your New Business 77
Chapter 12 Defining Your Niche 84
Chapter 13 Finding Customers... 90

Section IV   **Building a Business**

Chapter 14 The Biography of a Business 95
Chapter 15 Building a Business Around a Patent........... 99
Chapter 16 Raising Money For Your New Business......108
Chapter 17 Building Your New Organization...............114
Chapter 18 Bringing in Investors...................................121
Chapter 19 Franchising 124

Section V   **Some Last Words...**

Chapter 20 Preparing to Get Started 130
Chapter 21 Preparing for Graduation 134
Appendices 137

Dedication

This book is dedicated to my dear and wonderful wife
and partner, Nancy, who has loved
and stood by me these 27
years. You never stopped caring for and helping me.
You deserve to have this first major publication
breakthrough dedicated to you;
it belongs to both of us.

Introduction

This volume is designed to help you recognize, organize and realize what God intended by sending you ideas in the first place, and to motivate you to keep trying until you better achieve those results which will improve the quality of life for you and for all humankind.

The body of this book is designed to inform and inspire you how to build a business around your new idea, when it arrives. Whatever the form of your new idea, this book is meant to you to take at least one weekly "baby" step toward advancing it. Throughout my life, I have found endless inspiration in studying the lives of other successful creators. So, each chapter will feature a case study of someone who, in my opinion, has set a good example.

You will first need some new ideas to develop, and then assess your own skill set and destiny and obtain assistance with your marketing plan and protecting your ideas—that's what the body of each chapter is designed to do.

The book is divided into five sections so that you easily begin the study wherever it is appropriate for you. Everyone can proceed at his or her own pace. I hope that you thoroughly enjoy this journey with us.

Michael Robert Davis
California, 2003

EDISON

CARVER

CURIE

EINSTEIN

Section I

Creative Ideas Can Change Your World!

Chapter One

In the Beginning...

C reativity is a gift from God. He is, after all, the ultimate Creator, and we are constantly reminded of His power through the things He has made. Since we are made in His image, it only follows that we too can be blessed with creativity if we seek it.

In Proverbs 8:12, God promises us this creativity:

I, wisdom, dwell with prudence and find out knowledge of witty inventions.

Surprised that God is interested in inventions? We shouldn't be because He desires to bless us abundantly. In John 1:16 it says, "From the fullness of his grace we have all received one blessing after another."

In fact, God wants our ideas to help others and has purposed for us to become successful by developing them. He is constantly showering creative solutions on the earth: ideas for new products, new businesses, new books, poems, music, and movies, and improved ideas for existing products, businesses, services, and ways to help people. In short, God desires to show us better ways to do everything and solutions to every problem faced by humankind. And there is plenty of evidence that the pace has picked up dramatically—witness all the new inventions of the last century.

Many of us pursue and develop our God-given ideas into successful innovations and solutions, but a large number of us unfortunately ignore or dismiss them because we really don't know how to proceed. Throughout the pages of this book, you'll find practical steps to take so that you *can* begin to use the creativity that God has placed within you.

Profile of an Idea Person

Can just anyone tap into divine sources of inspiration? Matthew 5:45 says, "That ye may be the children of your Father which is in heaven: for he maketh his sun to rise on the evil and on the good, and sendeth rain on the just and on the unjust." In other words, in God's mercy, He allows ideas to rain on *everyone*.

At first glance, thought, it would seem that successful idea people were born with a natural talent for thinking of new and wonderful things, but when we examine their lives, we see that they had to work hard to make these ideas become real.

For example, Frank Lloyd Wright, the famous architect, set up a drafting table in his bedroom so that when fresh ideas came into his mind during the night, he could easily get up and write them down. He made himself available so that when the ideas came to him, he would not lose them.

I work with an inventor—let's call him "Fred"—who comes from a small town in Kentucky. Ideas kept coming to Fred in many different forms, and he was faithful in writing them down in a standard type of laboratory book. One idea was for a song that he wrote, which was later made famous by a well-known country western singer.

About 25 years ago, Fred began thinking about fossil fuel emissions after an acid rain cloudburst destroyed much of the new foliage on his land. Though he had no petroleum engineering training (but was good with chemical compositions), he decided to go to the library to begin studying the components of acid rain, vehicle emissions, and the worsening environmental situation.

As a result, several of Fred's energy-related discoveries permitted him to raise his family in grand style. Eventually his biggest discovery and patent were stolen by an untrustworthy partner. This was a very painful experience for Fred, so his son, who has a very good business mind, joined him about four years ago to help protect him from unscrupulous business people. As they worked together, Fred devised a completely new method for reducing fuel emissions at a lower cost than ever before. Although Fred's previous 20 or so inventions had provided him with a good income, this new patent application proved to have even greater commercial potential and appeal. This one, in other words, contained the "mother-lode."

We helped Fred to bring in several offers of venture capital funding in the millions of dollars and assisted him

4

in presenting licensing opportunities to major global oil companies. Fred's large chunk of stock in those companies has become worth a lot of money these days.

Fred loves God and is constantly on the lookout for fresh ideas and inspiration. He prays for daily direction on what to work on, whom to partner with, and for answers to scientific and commercial questions. In response to Thomas Edison's observation that creativity consisted of 1% inspiration and frequent 20-hour days, Fred asserts that his success is "50% inspiration, and 50% follow-through."

Fred's newer inventions are better than ever, with broad commercial appeal, and coming at a faster rate than before. If he had a laboratory assistant and an in-house patent attorney, he says he could file up to 100 patent applications a year. At that rate, in ten years, Fred might achieve Edison's accomplishment of 1093 patented inventions.

Fred's example teaches us that there is more to success than just receiving ideas. We must become good stewards of the ideas that come to us.

A wealthy entrepreneur from Georgia stated confidently that the more of himself and his business he gave to God, the more that God blessed him through commercially profitable ideas. Albert Einstein himself said, "ideas come from God." Although Einstein appeared not to claim a personal relationship with God, he still credited the final key piece of the Special Theory of Relativity to Him. We will explore this idea further in a later chapter.

Dr. John Avanzini, a good friend of mine, is fond of saying, "one new thought or idea can literally change your life in a split second!" We should not be afraid to ask God many questions that we have concerning everyday life and the problems we face because He likes to answer them. One mentor of mine told me to go to sleep asking a particular question, such as, "Where and whom should I go and see next to help me solve this particular problem?" Or, "What is my next step?" Frequently, the answer has come to me within 24 hours.

The following is an excerpt from an excellent book, entitled *101+ Ways God Talks*, by Sandy Warner (www.thequickenedword.com). This book has really opened my eyes to all the ways that God tries to communicate with us every minute of every day.

> Often we have ideas and do not recognize them as separate from ourselves. Sometimes we think we had a brilliant flash of genius when it really was the Lord. He is wonderful to speak rational, logical ideas into our lives. They are like short power-packed sentences.

> Our history [that of the United States] is founded upon inventors' sudden flashes of genius. They awakened in the morning with new ideas. Or, when they least expected it, they found answers in a simple thought, perhaps while doing something else. Brilliant and simple people alike have been inspired by the Holy Spirit with genius ideas. It is

comforting to know that the Holy Spirit is bigger than an IQ!

One day I was praying about needing another filing cabinet; the problem was that we had no practical space for one. My husband said, "Why don't you just clean out the ones we have?" Brilliant idea! Would you believe after 20 years of collecting, I threw away a 4-foot pile of paper? Not only did I find the answer to my filing needs, but in the process of throwing things away, I found some important material I needed for publishing my book. Thank You, Lord, for inspired insight.

Sandy's last practical example, described above, is something else that has been on my heart. We aren't just talking about breakthrough inventions, discoveries, songs, or novels here. Wisdom also finds out daily, practical solutions to all our problems––large and small––many of which we will not file patents on. Ideas come to us, in all shapes and sizes, throughout the night and day.

We know that new ideas are being showered down every day on everyone, but do we know why? Does one person have an advantage over another in the idea department? Why do some people pick them up and others not? How can we make ourselves more receptive to good ideas?

Frequently, we become aware of a need not presently being met that could benefit from a new or better device. For example, the aluminum can pop-top opener was invented by an average person looking for an easier way to open his beverages. Then, there are those who constantly seek out new discoveries, primarily for the purpose of commercial advantage. These people are poised to seek out other people's new ideas and evaluate them. Some professional investors, venture capitalists, and people we call business "angels" fall into this category. Many businesses and new divisions are formed through the investments of these people.

Bearing this in mind, what can we do to attune ourselves better to receive good new ideas? There are many things, of course; but I want to highlight several of them here:

1. Give to God first. Give God your self, your time, affections, mind, and money. One fantastically successful entrepreneur told many people his secret: the more he gave to God, the more ideas God gave him, which he incorporated into his rapidly growing business.

2. Keep communication lines open with God. Tune into the divine frequency, take notes, jot down ideas, daydream a lot, and use an idea journal.

3. Keep your day job. A wise entrepreneur and former president of a Fortune 500 company gave me this advice: "Support yourself 30-40 hours a week, and use evenings and Saturdays to develop new ideas, companies, and income." That advice has worked well for me over the years. Try working a little harder and a lot smarter.

Case Study:
The George Washington Carver Story

It was indeed the lowly peanut that made George Washington Carver a national folk hero in the United States and eventually famous worldwide. He personally discovered 300 uses for the peanut as a southern crop, and 100 uses each for the soybean and the pecan.

He measured his success by the amount of service that he rendered to African-Americans in the southeastern U.S. He turned down today's equivalent of one million dollars per year to work with Thomas Edison, and instead endured criticism and hardship to lead the Agriculture Department at Tuskegee Institute, dedicating himself to the higher education of African-Americans.

The aspects of George Washington Carver's life that impact me most are:

- He was so grateful to God and inspired by Him so much of the time that it humbles me.
- He overcame much adversity, poverty, racism, jealousy, and misunderstanding that it staggers the mind. His mother was kidnapped and disappeared. His father and sisters died prematurely, and he was weak and sickly himself.
- After being accepted by a college, he spent most of his money on his enrollment and transportation. When he arrived, the faculty realized he was an African American and rejected him.

- Finally accepted by Simpson College, he was eight years behind other white students.
- His primary motivation to leave the security of the farm and pursue more education was Christ's parable of the talents. As the "plant doctor" (his farm nickname), he felt that he was responsible to God to cultivate his talent through research.

Carver single handedly revolutionized southern agriculture, which was devastated by war, over farming, and the boll weevil, and convinced most farmers eventually to switch to the crop-rotation method.

I could talk about many other obvious things in Carver's life: his amazing testimony before Congress, his charity to needy townspeople, his discovery of mayonnaise, wood stain, meat tenderizer, and many other useful products. But I would rather examine a letter that he wrote explaining his prayer life and fellowship with God:

My prayers seem to be more of an attitude than anything else. I ask the Great Creator silently and often many times per day to permit me to speak to Him through the three great kingdoms of this world, which He has created—the animal, mineral and plant kingdoms – their relations to each other, to us, our relations to them, and the Great God Who made all of us. I ask Him often momently (moment by moment) to give me wisdom, understanding and bodily strength to do His will——hence I am asking and receiving all the time.

Very sincerely yours,
G.W. Carver

May we, like George Washington Carver, ask for and receive new ideas and discoveries all the time!

Recommended Activity: I remember reading a book on adult creativity in which the author wrote of carrying crayons around to stimulate his innovation and doodling, and recommended that others do the same. I've tried it and found that it's a good idea: it's freeing and fun. What does your idea look like? Can you draw it? Why not give it a try!

Chapter Two

Valuable Opportunities

A dmittedly, not all of us can be like Fred in the previous chapter, but Fred started out with one idea that he was faithful to pursue. If we are faithful with even one idea, then God will give us more. We don't know in advance which ideas will be successful, either commercially or in other terms; but our faithfulness and action will create further opportunities for us. It we are faithful to God and the ideas that He gives us, we will be capable of similar and greater accomplishments.

Another key to making the most of our opportunities is to identify our strengths and weaknesses. Realizing that he was weak in business negotiations and transactions, Fred strengthened himself by adding competent people around him in administration, finance, accounting, marketing and business development. (See Section III on the Nuts and Bolts of Business.) We can do the same thing. The biggest challenge that we face in pursuing our ideas is taking that first step––and taking regular steps thereafter.

There are many ways to profit commercially from

your ideas, but you may have to experiment with different business models until you find the one that's right for you.

There is a lot of good business, entrepreneurial, and innovative literature to read and get ideas from (some ideas for helpful magazines and resources are listed in the Appendices), and there are local seminars and classes you can attend. These are valuable opportunities to begin networking with other entrepreneurs and inventors.

But, in addition to everything else you do, please become convinced that God wants to show, reveal, and manifest completely unique ways for you to profit from these ideas. As He tells us in Isaiah 48:17:

> *Thus saith the Lord, thy Redeemer, the Holy One of Israel; I am the Lord thy God which teacheth thee to profit, which leadeth thee by the way that thou shouldest go.*

The more that you believe God desires to help you on your journey, the easier it becomes for you to take small, but daily steps into the unknown. If you don't have a specific idea right now for an invention, service, process or book, then read this material to understand the future steps you will need to take when you do receive one. Then go through each chapter, do the work, and answer each question. I guarantee that you won't be disappointed with the end results!

Whatever the form of your God-sent idea, this book is intended to motivate you to take at least one weekly step towards advancing it. The reflections contained in these chapters will follow my own journey of pursuing the ideas that God gives to me, reviewing the progress made during the week, and regrouping as needed over the weekend—ready to charge hard again on Monday morning.

As I have shared some of these suggestions with others, many of them have taken the first steps to pursue their ideas. For example, a poet began writing a special type of poetry and is now looking for the right artist to illustrate several pieces and bookmarks for publication. Two inventors drew one-page diagrams of their ideas to accompany provisional patent applications (recommended by the Patent Office). And one innovative toy inventor finally broke through and sewed a prototype of her toy idea, enabling her to begin taking orders for it from niche boutique toy stores.

My cousin, a hotel entrepreneur, wants to build a new resort without traditional bank financing. Because visualization is so important to the success of her idea, my first recommendation was for her to obtain an artist's conceptual rendering of how the resort might look to potential investors. She has already taken this first step and has begun using it to make the proper contacts. If you can visualize something, then, frequently, you can find the means to obtain the financing and help to bring it to pass.

If your idea is for a novel, then your path will take you into developing your plot, setting, and characters. Some authors go into great detail creating their characters with sketches and notes. J.R.R. Tolkein, for example, created an entire history of another world as the basis for writing his famous Lord of the Rings trilogy.

There are various ways to begin using the creative ideas God has given to you. Just don't be afraid to begin. The following are the various obstacles that you may need to overcome and the names of some successful people who did it:

- You're never too old to innovate. Think of the Kentucky Colonel––Harland Sanders.
- You're never too young to invent things. The youngest U.S. patent was awarded to a four-year-old girl from Texas; the Wright brothers dreamed as children of being able to fly; the inventor of the television got the technical idea at aged 14.
- You're never too poor to change the world. Think of George Washington Carver and Mother Teresa.
- You're never too oppressed to design new things. Mr. Rubix, who lived in the former Eastern European bloc, invented the Rubix cube.
- You're never too undereducated or inexperienced to help mankind. (See the story of Ruth Fertel below.)
- You're never too handicapped to inspire others. Think of Helen Keller.

Basically, you're never too anything to pursue your ideas and dreams. And as Paul says in Romans 8:31: "If God is for you, who can be against you?"

Case Study: The Ruth Fertel Story

Ruth Fertel of New Orleans was almost 40 years old when she found herself in quite a predicament. The divorced single mother of two sons, Ruth found herself stuck in a dead-end medical laboratory position with little hope for growth or promotion, and not enough money to send her boys to college. She scanned the local newspaper classified ads in desperation.

Ruth's eyes were drawn to an advertisement for a small, neighborhood restaurant called "Chris Steak House." Knowing nothing about the food service industry at all but acting on a hunch, Ruth Fertel borrowed $22,000 against her house to purchase the business. She added her name to the one existing, creating "Ruth's Chris Steak House," and perfected an unusual way of preparing the meat. Site seared the best corn-fed beef at 1800° and then quickly served the steaks still sizzling on the plate. An excellent product combined with a comfortable atmosphere made her steakhouse appealing to businesspeople who found her restaurant conducive to closing and celebrating deals. It wasn't long before she added a second successful location in Baton Rouge and so on. By 2001, there were over 80 locations of Ruth's Chris Steak House worldwide doing over $300 million in annual revenue. Whether in Hong Kong or Dallas or San Francisco, businesspeople knew they could count on Ruth's chain for an enjoyable, higher-end dining experience with guests and clients.

The lessons that I see represented in Ruth Fertel's life are:

- She was stuck in what she perceived as a dead-end job and wasn't fulfilling her dream and passion. As a 40-year old breadwinner for her family, she made a bold move to change those dynamics.

- She knew so little about the restaurant business that, unless her banker had helped her, she wouldn't have had enough supplies to open her doors. Yet, that didn't stop her.

- There is an amazing power and value in developing a brand name and trademarked concept: Ruth developed her business from minimum profits from one restaurant to over $300 million in revenues from 80 locations per year.

- The more than 1000-fold return on investment that she received: from $22,000 to more than $22 million in net worth over 35 years.

- She progressed from being a cash-strapped single mom to what many described as a classic example of the American dream.

Recommended Reading: *Anointed for Business* by Ed Silvoso is an excellent new book about how readers can use their influence in the marketplace to change the world. You can purchase it at www.harvestevan.org.

Chapter Three

Benefits of Developing Your Ideas

This book is all about ideas and creativity and the joy and benefit that they can bring to you and others. It is hard to describe the sense of well being that comes from successfully receiving and executing an idea.

Let's take a close look at just some ways in which you will benefit from taking some risks and developing your ideas:

Emotionally – There is an excellent sense of accomplishment that comes from working on your own ideas. Working on someone else's ideas is important training and pays the bills, but there is nothing to compare with successfully developing your own.

Mentally – We only use a small portion of our mental gifting, and most of us develop a lifestyle that allows us to live on "cruise control." Most of the time we are not mentally challenged to think creatively and solve real problems.

Working on your own ideas will challenge you to daily seeking answers to "what step should I take next?" and solutions for the problems you come up against.

Physically – We know that good enzymes and chemicals are released through our bodies when we are content and fulfilled. If there are some good laughs and enjoyment along the way, so much the better, for they are good for the body.

Spiritually – If we are in tune with God and receptive to His messages, encouragement, and ideas for us, then there can be a tremendous sense of filling the void and vacuum within each of us. There is nothing else––material goods, money, drugs, alcohol, or sex––that can successfully meet that internal need.

Materially – If we are faithfully executing our day jobs and additionally working on our own ideas, then our basic needs should be covered. There may not be much left over, especially in the beginning, but we are sowing into our future and the potential payoff of our ideas.

Benevolently – If we continue to look out for others in need along the way, then we will be rewarded. Even when John D. Rockefeller, Sr., was earning very little as a clerk in Cleveland, Ohio, he still regularly shared what he had with those in greater need. If we are faithful in a little, then we will be faithful in a lot and God will bless our faithfulness.

Case Study: Albert Einstein

Albert Einstein received an idea at the age of 26, now called the theory of relativity. He came from a poor Jewish family in Italy. He did not perform well in school, partly because he was creative, asked a lot of questions, and challenged the prevailing theories of physics under a stern European educational system that taught only by rote learning. He and his future wife finished last in their college class in their physics specialty.

No one wanted to hire Einstein as a junior professor intern or even to sign off on his doctoral thesis. Einstein was so desperate that he seriously considered an alternative office job in the insurance business as a means of supporting his young family! The Swiss government did not want to grant him citizenship, and he was fired from a teaching position after only four months. It was only through one of his close friends, who recognized Einstein's genius and went to bat for him at the Swiss patent office, that Einstein was reluctantly given a lowly clerk position.

Was Einstein a good patent clerk? Although his mind was elsewhere, preoccupied on solving the theoretical questions dogging him day and night, and his knowledge of mechanical engineering was weak, Einstein did execute his duties as a patent clerk in a competent manner. He was able to more quickly figure out the novelty of a patent application than his colleagues. As a result, his boss gave him a nice raise and overlooked some of his imperfections. The lowly clerk opportunity was only a temporary foundation from which he built and published his theories while supporting a young family.

Lessons that we can learn from the life of Albert Einstein include the following:

1) Einstein looked to God for inspiration, solutions, and ideas. One biographer was amazed upon verifying this quote from Einstein himself: "Ideas come from God. You cannot command the idea to come, it will come when it's good and ready."

2) Be particularly open to receiving ideas at night and write them down, or if you are a musician, record them. Have your notebook or recorder handy. It's one way of saying, "I'm ready when you are, God."

3) Find and form a close circle of positive, encouraging friends who promote one another. This is what Einstein did, calling the group his "Olympia Academy." Or, find one like-minded person and create an "idea buddy" system.

4) Look for a job that allows you to develop your ideas and yet still meet your current obligations. Friends can often help you find the right interim position.

5) We have to overcome significant adversity to find our highest and best use on this earth. Some of the hurdles that Albert Einstein had to overcome in order to become the world's most prominent scientist in his generation were: poverty, anti-Semitism, discrimination, lack of parental support, jealousy of his teachers, and the entrenched viewpoints of contemporary scientists.

Which of these five lessons can help you this coming week in moving your idea forward? Do you have several friends to encourage you to be your best? Why not form your equivalent of the Olympia Academy, discussing ideas and projects over coffee? If you could modify your present position or situation to give you several more hours per week, what would you do differently?

Case Study: Horatio Alger

Horatio Alger, Jr., was the author of over 100 books that inspired young people from the post-Civil War era through the end of the 19th century. His novels of courage, faith, and hard work captured the imagination of generations of young Americans and gave them a model of hope and promise in the face of hardships.

Born in Revere, Massachusetts, in 1832, he was the son of a pastor who instilled a strong religious belief in him. A Phi Beta Kappa graduate of Harvard, Alger studied under Henry Wadsworth Longfellow and intended to become a poet. He worked at one time as a teacher and a newspaper correspondent for the Boston Transcript and the New York Sun. Affected by asthma, Alger was rejected by the Union Army and eventually became a minister on Cape Cod.

Alger wrote more than 120 books with the inspiring theme of "onward and upward." He began writing his rags-to-riches tales just after the Cavil War, and patterned the hero of his book, Ragged Dick, after the homeless newsboys and bootblacks he observed in his New York neighborhood. The heroes of his books almost always were moral, brave, generous, kind, diligent, industrious, and persevering. His novels told everyone, no matter how poor, orphaned, or powerless, that they could succeed if then did their best, persevered in it, and always tried to do the right thing. He told them that success was earned through hard work and right action. He trumpeted the doctrine of achieving success through self-reliance, self-discipline, decency, and honesty.

Alger's books were always best-sellers and almost every home, school, and church library in America boasted a large collection of them. More than 250 million copies of his books have been sold worldwide, and through his body of work, Alger captured the spirit of a nation and helped to clarify it.

He became the unlikeliest candidate ever to receive the title, "The Most Published American Author," with one-quarter billion books sold when the U.S. population was approximately 50 million strong—–an average of five books per U.S. resident! What a strong influence Horatio Alger had on the psyche of a growing nation! Alger's teaching of equal opportunity for all, overcoming every obstacle through hard work, and progressing "from rags to riches" have become synonymous with the United States of America.

Recommended Reading: *Molder of Dreams* by Guy Rice Doud and Tony Campolo, Ph.D. Campolo is a Christian professor who is not afraid to tackle difficult issues. Bold in his stance and approach, he has authored a number of good books. *Molder of Dreams* is my favorite because of the subject matter: helping to mold others' dreams and forwarding their hopes. Guy Doud, National Teacher of the year in 1986, and Dr. Campolo have written an entertaining, moving and autobiographical book that asserts the power people have to mold one another's dreams and influence the hopes of others.

Chapter Four

Let's Go Out There
and Do Something

What is the next important step for you to take? Is there something that you could do this afternoon and move you closer to your goal? Is there something that you could do early next week? For your next step, let me make one suggestion: Do something...do anything!

Some readers have already received enough direction—from me, from this book and from God—to go out and start something new. That next step can be to create, to innovate, to write, to paint, or to build a new business. We're on a journey, and I want to encourage you to take that next bold step into the unknown.

Let me give you an example from my life. I was bogged down editing a book. Fifty thousand words are a lot to double-check and improve, and I really wanted to work on my next two manuscripts in progress. But I had to get the diskette to the publisher soon. My AutoRecover feature had lost all my writing from the previous day through a computer glitch. I could not get through to my publisher on the telephone or by email, so I didn't sleep well that night and suffered for it the next day.

So what was my next step? Our enemy, the devil, will occasionally step in and try to stop you dead in your tracks. So how did I overcome this potential deathblow attempt? I call it buoyancy, resiliency, perseverance, and faith. It was the ability to bounce back stronger in resolve than ever, along with an internal fortitude of spirit that says, "Every time that you try to push me down, I'm going to come back twice as hard as before." The story had a happy ending. The diskette made it to the printer, and I'm still on schedule. May you bounce back stronger than ever and overcome the forces of inertia as you begin your new adventure.

Case Study: The Alabama Cake Lady

This is a true story, and one that has become legendary as it has been retold many times across the world. There was a poor lady in Alabama whose husband had died and who found herself in difficult financial straits. She was watching a fundraiser for a particular charity on television, and she heard God say, "I would like you to give $30,000 to that charity." Now, most of us would have protested loudly and complained about our present state of lack. Many would have shrugged off that suggestion and muttered to themselves about the bills still needing to be paid. But not the Alabama Cake Lady! She said, "That would be so nice. It would be wonderful to do that." Can you believe her attitude? She was filled with hope and faith.

This lady had a special family recipe for making moist delicious cakes. It was a secret recipe that used the squash vegetable for taste, texture, and moisture. So, she made several of these cakes and took them down to the local truck stop and diner in her town. She asked the restaurant manager if he would buy one and offer it to his diners. He flatly said no, but a customer, sitting within earshot, spoke up and said to the manager, "If you will carry these cakes, I will eat a piece or two each visit and take one to go. I've eaten her cakes before and they are really good!" The manager was convinced, and she began supplying him with her special cakes.

Her business grew and grew. She recruited some friends to help her bake and deliver these cakes to the businesses in town. Her reputation, and that of her cakes, continued to spread to the outlying areas. Her fortunes greatly changed over several short years.

I have a close friend who met the Alabama Cake Lady in person at that charity's annual telethon event several years later. She was wearing an expensive dress, fancy shoes and nice jewelry, and the well-dressed gentleman standing next to her was her chauffeur! She now owned an apartment house complex in town, where she lived in good style on the top floor in her furnished penthouse. She was at the telethon to present her annual check for $30,000—which she had been doing for a number of years—ever since she had first responded with, "That would be so nice!" and not "I can't because I'm broke."

God frequently shares "potentialities" with us, but we miss the cues. He wanted the Alabama Cake Lady to prosper so much that writing an annual check for $30,000 wouldn't be difficult for her to do. God loves the unusual response, the uncommon reply, and the one in a million attitude. Let us become extra-ordinary idea people this week, this month, this year.

Recommended Reading: Enjoy some of the magazines listed in Appendix J. Read them, mark them up (if you own them), and see if any new ideas come to you as a result. *I Wrote This Book on Purpose,* by John Stanko, PhD. Also, his weekly "The Monday Memo" email encouragement service (free), both available through www.purposequest.com. I also highly recommend two additional books for your ongoing education: *The Rich God's Guide To Starting a Business,* which I am co-authoring with John Avanzini and Patrick Ondrey (Abel Press); and also, *The McGraw-Hill Guide to Starting Your Own Business: A Step-By-Step Blueprint for the First-Time Entrepreneur,* by Stephen C. Harper.

(Speaking of books, here is an idea to save money when you shop. If you want to buy a particular book on Amazon.com, then keep clicking for more product details until you get access to used book information for that title. For example, you can sometimes buy a used copy for as little as 22 cents plus shipping to your home or office. I have never been disappointed yet, buying a used book from an Amazon four-star rated used bookseller. Soon, you'll be buying good, used copies for less than ten cents on the retail dollar!)

Section II

Intellectual Property

29

Chapter Five

Patents

I deas come in all shapes and sizes. So many, in fact, that people who might not consider themselves to be entrepreneurs will be surprised to find out just how many possibilities there are.

In today's world, one of the first steps we need to take is to protect our ideas. The fact is that many people get the same ideas at about the same time in different locations on this globe. It's possible that God chooses to shower the same idea all over the earth simultaneously and without preference or prejudice to any particular person or nation. With so many people receiving new ideas at the same time, protection of those ideas is more important than ever. One time I was with a business couple who had come up with a new idea and shared it in a seminar. The leader asked them, "Have you submitted your idea yet?"––an important step that must not be overlooked.

A good idea should be protected by a patent or you will run the risk of another person using that idea and reaping much of what could have been *your* profit. A vivid example of this is a certain company in New England that received a lot of publicity for the generosity of its founder and owner towards his employees during the reconstruction of their burned-down facility. It was a solid company that treated its employees well. Unfortunately, the formerly successful textile company eventually had to begin Chapter 11 reorganization proceedings (a form of bankruptcy), primarily because it never obtained patent protection for its main ingenious idea, which, in turn, permitted its competitors to catch up and overtake it.

Intellectual property is a type of property created by our imagination––our ideas––and takes various forms that can be protected by law. The chapters in this section will look at the major types: patents, trademarks, trade secrets, and family recipes.

What Is a Patent?

A patent for an invention is the grant of a property right to the inventor, issued by the Patent and Trademark Office. The term of a new patent is 20 years from the date on which the application for the patent was filed in the United States or, in special cases, from the date an earlier related application was filed, subject to the payment of maintenance fees. U.S. patent grants are effective only within the U.S., its territories, and its possessions.

The right conferred by the patent grant is, in the language of the statute and of the grant itself, "the right to exclude others from making, using, offering for sale, or selling" the invention in the United States or "importing" the invention into the United States. Within the limits of what you request of the United States Patent Office (hopefully, in as broad terms as possible) and what they eventually approve (probably somewhat narrower), you have the right to prevent and exclude others from directly competing with your invention for a period of 20 years.

Keep in mind that patents are not perfect protection for your idea. Think of them as a white picket fence around your property—they look nice, and they discourage trespassers. Of course, the broader the fence, the more territory it protects, and the more property that you really own.

Patents can be expensive and take a lot work to develop and register internationally but have the potential to be very lucrative for their 20-year span.

The following are three categories of patents:

Utility (90%)—protects useful processes, machines, articles of manufacture, and compositions of matter. Examples: fiber optics, computer hardware, medications;

Design (9%)—guard the unauthorized use of new, original, and ornamental designs for articles of manufacture. The look of an athletic shoe, a bicycle helmet, and the Star Wars characters are all protected by design patents;

Plant (1%)—the way we protect invented or discovered asexually reproduced plant varieties. Hybrid tea roses, Silver Queen corn, and Better Boy tomatoes are all types of plant patents.

Legal Help

The first step for an invention, in my opinion, is to meet with a leading patent law firm in your area that has specific expertise with your type of technology or industry. For example, high-tech communications is very different, engineering-wise, from a new skincare product, for example. The ideal law firm will have an excellent patent litigation record that will tend to scare off would-be patent offenders.

Time is of the essence. Some major inventions have been disputed tin the basis of several hours' difference between who filed what and when! Remember: ideas hit different people at about the same time, so whoever gets to the patent office first has a great advantage.

Gordon Gould was the first to think of a way to make a laser, but another group beat him to the U.S. patent office. However, since Gould kept good laboratory notes, he eventually prevailed in court 30 years later and became the millionaire that he deserved to become. Despite this, however, his life would have been much easier had he been the first to the patent office.

Another important question to ask yourself is what your finances will allow you to do. I can take several thousand dollars to get started on the first patent application. You may need to draw on the financial resources of your own family, relatives, and friends in order to get started.

Once you find a patent law firm, you will want to get an estimate of charges and costs. Find out what the average hourly billing rate will be, and what decisions will have to be made regarding domestic and international patent rights over the first three years. Be sure you are comfortable with the attorney with whom you will be working.

The first thing that he/she will do is a patent search. A simple patent search can generally be conducted for several hundred dollars, and you can assist by searching patents via the Internet (see instructions later in this chapter). Keep in mind that you want as broad a patent as possible—let a federal examiner narrow your claims, not you. Be as general as your attorney will allow you to be, and remember that time is of the essence here, since other people are typically entertaining similar thoughts and ideas like yours. It's a race to get that first application filed.

Provisional Patents

When money is lacking and very difficult to raise, a provisional patent filing gives you one-year "patent pending" protection while you seek to take your product or service to market and raise additional working capital with a good marketing and business plan.

Each year the U.S. Patent Office issues about 175,000 patents from approximately 360,000 total applications. A new patent is issued, on average, every six minutes— but only a few ever hit the marketplace. Interestingly enough, this number is up dramatically from the 60 or so applications per year that Thomas Jefferson personally reviewed as the first head of our Patent Office. A spokesperson from the patent office cautions us, "You may come up with a wonderful idea, but so many don't do their homework and [they do not] devise a marketing and business plan. The patents themselves are not cheap—costing about $4,000 on average."

So, you can see that it sometimes makes sense to go with a provisional patent to give you time to get your marketing and business plan going. Filing fees average only about $80 for an individual or small business. How much to spend initially on attorney patent search and preparation fees is your biggest question here. The answer that makes the most sense to me is to spend as much as you and your investors think is prudent. If that is $100, then that is what you spend. If it is $2000, then use it wisely and don't overspend initially. In my opinion, the ability to advertise "patent-pending" is a very strong selling point to raising capital and/or trying to license your idea or bring it to market.

There are good books, resources, and software readily available to help you write a terrific business and marketing plan, so I am not going to reinvent the wheel here. I am, however, going to highly encourage you to do your homework and focus on an Executive Summary and Marketing Plan, because marketing your product is critical and overlooked by most inventive people.

The primary benefits of a provisional patent are:

1) It provides simplified filing with a lower initial investment with one full year to assess the invention's commercial potential before

committing to the higher cost of filing and prosecuting a non-provisional "formal" application for patent.

2) It establishes an official United States patent application filing date for the invention.

3) It permits one-year's authorization to use a "Patent Pending" notice in connection with the invention—which, in my experience, is extremely important.

4) It enables immediate commercial promotion of the invention with greater security against having the invention stolen.

The Provisional Patent Application's (PPA) initial advantage over filing a Formal Patent Application (FPA) is summarized below:

		PPA	FPA
1.	Amount of USPTO filing fee?	$80	$370
2.	Provides "Patent Pending" status?	Yes	Yes
3.	Declaration not required?	Yes	
4.	Difficult "Claims" section not required?	Yes	
5.	Guaranteed for one year?	Yes	
6.	Not examined for patentability by USPTO?	Yes	
7.	Number of hours of legal time required?	0-1+	10-20+

Also, for the cost of one hour of an attorney's time, there are software programs that can prepare your PPA for you. Do a Google Internet search (go to www.google.com, then type in "Provisional Patent Applications") to find which one might be best for you. You'll want to be sure it will assist you in writing a brief written description and summary of the invention as well as a simple diagram, if possible.

If you don't have the money for a patent attorney now, then you will need to spend some time on the Internet looking at issued patents on your field of invention. This will allow you to acquaint yourself with the words, phrases, concepts and other unique aspects of patent terminology. Then, when you have enough money to see a patent attorney, you will be that much more knowledgeable and helpful in the patent application drafting process.

Internet Patent Searches

Go to www.uspto.gov, an excellent user-friendly web site. (My compliments to the Patent and Trademark Office for a job well done!)

- Click on "Patents" on the left side
- Click on "SEARCH Patents"
- In the box labeled "Term 1:", type an initial search phrase describing your invention; (If the years 1996--2002 are not the period that you want to search, then make that correction)
- Hit the "Search" button
- Repeat with different phrases until you fine-tune those that best describe your potential patent application. Study their descriptions contained in the "Abstract" sections at the top of each issued patent.

How to File a PPA:

In addition to the description of your invention, the provisional application must include:

- All drawings necessary to understand the invention
- Names of all inventors
- The appropriate filing fee (approximately $80 for individual inventors)
- A cover sheet that identities the invention.

International Patent Coverage: Patent Cooperation Treaty (PCI)

Again, I don't want to convey the idea that patents are simple or easy—they are more complicated, expensive, and extensive than trademarks or copyrights, as you will soon discover in the next chapters. Many patent attorneys have engineering backgrounds for a good reason. Patents can be quite complicated. You will need a good patent attorney to prepare your full-blown Formal Patent Application (FPA) and to pursue your international rights thereafter. Ask him/her to explain how PCT filings work overseas, and the costs and timing involved with them.

Many patents never earn enough to pay back their original cost, so be careful how you spend money here. I like to use investor's money for patent development because they help to share the risk. If they like the idea enough to invest in it, then you have earned the right to use their money to fully patent and commercialize your product or service. But don't just run out and spend thousands of dollars just to say that you have a patent. You and your advisors—–not your patent attorney—–must assess and weigh the likely commercial rewards against the initial costs. Provisional patent applications allow you to do just that in a cost-effective way for one year.

An important note to all inventors: Be sure to keep good notes during your inventing process, as these may become important if date of discovery ever becomes an issue. Use a standard Laboratory Notebook as a daily or weekly discipline to help protect and organize your discoveries.

Case Study: Thomas Jefferson, the Father of the U.S. Patent Office

There are some things that I particularly like about Thomas Jefferson. It was at his request that Lewis and Clark explored the western wilderness. He invented all kinds of things for his own personal convenience and benefit at Monticello: a revolving serving door, revolving chair and table, and the moldboard of a plow among other useful things. He negotiated the Louisiana Purchase and served as our third American president. Even though he is known for brilliantly drafting our Declaration of Independence, he was not a gifted public speaker. He was more of a writer than an orator.

At the time of the American Revolution, attorneys and judges had developed the existing British system for patents over time, but the government did not regulate it, and it was very inefficient and fairly expensive.

Extensive litigation on Watt's 1796 patent for steam engines in England established the important principles that valid patents could be granted for improvements in a known machine, and for ideas or principles. Up until that time, any prospective patentee had to present a petition to no less than seven offices, paying fees at each one. (This procedure was described in exaggerated form, and somewhat derisively, by Charles Dickens in his spoof, "A Poor Man's Tale of a Patent"––where Dickens' inventor visits a total of 34 offices.)

So, the new nation––to some degree suspicious of things British––needed a better model for a national patenting process that was fair, reasonable, and efficient. The first American Patent Act was passed by Congress in 1790 and called for the Secretary of State to head the new Patent Office. As Secretary of State, Thomas Jefferson tried to develop a system that worked for the benefit of all––both the inventors and the consumers. He saw two challenges: how to foster innovation and get these new inventions out to as many people as possible and how to modify the European principle of monopoly so that it would benefit everyone.

The solution that was eventually developed was that patents would benefit the owner for a period of 20 years––after that, all society had free access to the ideas. (Trademarks and copyrights, on the other hand, were scheduled to benefit their owners for much longer periods of time.)

Jefferson's first test for judging inventions was that they had to be useful. Next, a patent would not be given to an existing invention built with a different material, or an application of something already invented. Also, in those days, a working model was required. (This is not necessarily needed by present day inventors.)

Being an inventor himself, Jefferson often insisted on testing each invention himself. His procedure was careful and time-consuming, which explains today's careful and time-consuming process at the United States Patent and Trademark Office. During his two-year term, he personally reviewed all 114 patent applications, and his office granted 67 patents. The most famous patent granted during his service was to Eli Whitney for the cotton gin. Jefferson wrote to Whitney:

> As the state of Virginia, of which I am, carries on household manufactures of cotton to a great extent, as I also do myself, and one of our great embarrassments is the clearing the cotton of the seed, I feel a considerable interest in the success of your invention for family use. Permit me therefore to ask information from you on these points:
>
> - Has the machine been thoroughly tried in the ginning of cotton, or is it as yet but a machine of theory?
> - What quantity of cotton has it cleaned on average of several days, and worked by hand and by how many hands?
> - What will be the cost of one of them made to be worked by hand?

Favorable answers to these questions would induce me to engage one of them to be forwarded to Richmond for me." ––Thomas Jefferson (November 16, 1793)

My observation of Thomas Jefferson is of someone who was a civic leader as well as being inventive and full of fresh ideas. You, too, can do more than you think! Let's be more than one-dimensional beings, with one gift and one forte, using 25% of our God-given creativity and brainpower. Let's strive this week to be, say, three-dimensional persons with several gifts and strengths using 70% of our God-given capacity! There is a promised place of both increased rest and more productivity in store for us, which we want to increasingly appropriate and enter.

Recommended Reading: *Patent It Yourself,* now in its 9th edition, is the world's best-selling patent book written by a patent attorney and former patent examiner. It thoroughly explains the patent process and copyrights and has all the forms (35) and instructions needed to patent a product in the United States. After checking out the details, buy it or borrow it from your local or college library.

Chapter Six

Trademarks

The next type of protection that we will discuss is the trademark. A "mark" is a unique name, logo, look, feel or sound used in marketplace trade. Trademarks protect words, names, symbols, sounds, or colors that distinguish goods and services. Unlike patents, trademarks can be renewed forever, as long as they are being used in business. The roar of the MGM lion, the pink of the insulation made by Owens-Corning (who uses the Pink Panther in advertising, by permission of its owner), the unique sound of a Harley-Davidson engine, and the shape of a Coca-Cola bottle are all familiar trademarks. A trademark may be claimed anytime by simply using the "TM" designation to alert the public to one's claim.

The next time you go into your local Starbucks outlet, look at the following trademarks listed on their price list:

Starbucks Iced Drinks®—–this is because most anything attached to an existing trademark is distinctive enough to warrant its own registration

Frappucino®––approved and registered
Tazo®––approved and registered
Venti™ (extra large size)––applied for and pending
Gold Coast Blend®––approved and registered
Yukon Blend®––approved and registered.

Simple Internet Searches
for U.S. Trademarks

Now let's have some fun and look at trademark filings with the United States Patent and Trademark Office (USPTO):

- Type in www.uspto.gov (this stands for United States Gov't. Patent & Trademark Office)
- Click on "Trademarks" on left-hand side
- Then click on "Search Trademarks (TESS):"
- In the center of the next page, hit "New User Form Search (Basic)" at the top of the available list
- On the next page, you see an open space entitled, "Search Term." Type in the basic word or phrase or idea that you want to check. Then hit "Submit Query" button;

> For example, type in the trade name, "Gillette." You should get 48 items listed,

- Click on the first one: "Gillette Comfort Glide Formula." You'll find that this trademark application was filed in November, 2000, and is still pending. That is why current cans of Gillette®

44

Foamy® with Comfort Glide Formula™ have a TM instead of an official R(egistered) symbol;

Study well-prepared applications like that one to learn a lot about your own needs and strategies for protecting your own names.

Helps for understanding the listings:

- Serial Number––the filed application reference number
- Registration Number––the approved Trademark Registration number
- Word Mark is the word(s) being applied for
- Live/Dead is the status of whether the application is still alive (pending) or dead (rejected or abandoned)

It's that simple! This can be a great idea tool for brainstorming your intellectual property approach giving you maximum protection for minimum expense. I've saved thousands of dollars by first thinking through my intellectual property goals, and then researching the trademarks of similar products myself. And you can, too!

For $335 plus the cost of some legal assistance, you might well be able, like Ruth Fertel (Ruth's Chris Steak Houses), to create a trademark eventually worth many millions of dollars. But remember this self-searching is no substitute for a trademark attorney conducting one of three different levels of searches on your proposed mark.

Although self-research is a very useful tool, even if you think the results of searching the USPTO databases are okay, do not assume that your mark can be registered there. After you file an application, the USPTO must do its own search and review, and might still refuse to register your mark. Be sure to consult a trademark attorney first if you have further questions.

A ™ means that the trademark has been applied for but not yet approved and issued. On the other hand, a ® means that the mark has been approved, issued and registered, with a specific USPTO registration number.

So we see that a trademark within the United States can be obtained for about $335 per category, it can be kept in force as long as it is being used in business, and you can do a lot of the internet searching yourself. That's a bargain in my book!

International Trademark Protection

International trademark treaties are generally ruled by the Paris Convention. In a layperson's language, this means that you generally have six months from when you file your U.S. trademark application in which to file in other major foreign countries in order to preserve your original filing date.

Check with your trademark attorney regarding the international IP situation. And yes, the European Community does have central filing for about 18 different countries with one application (this does not include the United Kingdom or Ireland––those must be separate applications).

Case Study: Walt Disney's Dreams

Walt Disney liked to take his daughters out on weekends to enjoy parks, amusements, and other good, clean fun places in Los Angeles. He was struck, however, by the general lack of entertainment options for them to visit. The more he thought about it, the more he began to dream of creating "The Happiest Place on Earth"—a place that he would love to take his own children. Walt traced the seeds of Disneyland to the Sunday mornings when he picked up his daughters at Sunday School and took them to an amusement park where they rode the merry-go-round and other attractions. He was repelled by the dirt, litter, and unfriendliness of such places, and knew he could do better.

Walt Disney grew up in Chicago but did not have an easy life. He moved west to Hollywood to make his mark on the new movie and television industries. His motion picture milestones were many, beginning with the birth of Mickey Mouse in the famous 1928 short titled "Steamboat Willie," which included synchronized sound on film for the first time in an animated motion picture.

He pioneered animation as a form for feature-length motion pictures with the creation of Snow White and the Seven Dwarfs and turned animation into a cinematic symphonic concert through Fantasia. He pioneered the creation of the multiplane camera, which recently earned him a place in the Inventors Hall of Fame.

During the late 1940s, Walt Disney began to design a theme park, and his dream began to take on new hope and potentiality. Walt's brother, Roy, helped him raise the needed money. Disney bought the property in southern California in the early 1950s and began to construct his ideas into real buildings and streets.

I'm reminded of a quote that I read by F. Buechner: "The place God calls you to is the place where your deep gladness and the world's deep hunger meet." For Walt Disney, his deep gladness sprang from a genuine desire to make people, especially children, happy. One of the world's great hungers is (and continues to be) for good, clean fun and family entertainment. Disneyland, featuring the Disney characters, indeed became for many visitors "the happiest place on earth."

The fact that Walt Disney succeeded so well is now reflected in additional subsequent locations in Orlando, Florida; near Paris, France; Tokyo, Japan; and next, Hong Kong. The present market value of The Walt Disney Company is approximately $50 billion! Who would have guessed that doodling and drawing a mouse could result in a market capitalization of $50 billion?

Where is the place that your great gladness and the world's great hunger intersect? Perhaps, over a hot cup of coffee or tea this weekend, you could reflect more on that vital question.

Recommended Activity: Pick up some famous name brand items lying around your residence or office, and do a little internet searching to acquaint yourself with some well-prepared trademark applications. Go to your pantry and study the trademarks. Product branding using trademarks creates tremendous value everywhere.

Recommended Reading: *The Revenge of Brand X: How to Build A Big Time Brand.* The best quote in this book is "Branding is not about getting your prospects to choose you over your competition; it's about getting your prospects to see you as the *only* solution to their problem (SM)."

Chapter Seven

Copyrights

If we've established one thing thus far in this book, it would be that protection costs money. At one point in time, RJR Nabisco had a hundred attorneys and in-house staff just to protect all their international trademarks. When I think about the potential cost of patent protection worldwide, and the time and money required to enforce trademarks around the globe, I can truly get excited about the international ease and lack of cost regarding copyrights.

A copyright is a form of protection provided to authors for "original works of authorship" including literary, dramatic, musical, artistic, and certain other intellectual works, both published and unpublished. The 1976 Copyright Act generally gives the owner of a copyright the exclusive right to reproduce the copyrighted work, to prepare derivative works, to distribute copies or recordings of the copyrighted work, to perform the copyrighted work publicly, and to display the copyrighted work publicly.

The copyright protects the *form* of expression rather than the *subject matter* of the writing. For example, a description of a machine could be copyrighted, but this would only prevent others from copying the description; it would not prevent others from writing a description of their own or from making and using the machine. Copyrights are registered by the Copyright Office of the Library of Congress (not the U.S. Patent and Trademark Office).

Copyright Protection

Copyright protection exists from the time the work is created in fixed form. The copyright immediately becomes the property of the author who created the work. Only the author or those deriving their rights through the author can rightfully claim copyright. In the case of works made for hire, the employer and not the employee is considered to be the author.

Copyright protects "original works of authorship" that are fixed in a tangible form of expression. The fixation need not be directly perceptible so long as it may be communicated with the aid of a machine or device. Copyright-able works include the following categories:

1) literary works;
2) musical works, including any accompanying words
3) dramatic works, including any accompanying music
4) pantomimes and choreographic works
5) pictorial, graphic, and sculptural works
6) motion pictures and other audiovisual works

7) sound recordings
8) architectural works

These categories should be viewed broadly. For example, computer programs and most "compilations" may be registered as "literary works," and maps and architectural plans may be registered as "pictorial, graphic, and sculptural works."

Copyright Secured Automatically

The way in which copyright protection is secured is frequently misunderstood. No publication, registration or other action in the Copyright Office is required to secure a copyright, but there are certain definite advantages to registration.

Copyright is automatically secured when the work is created, and a work is "created" when it is fixed in a copy or recording for the first time. "Copies" are material objects from which a work can be read or visually perceived either directly or with the aid of a machine or device, such as books, manuscripts, sheet music, film, videotape, or microfilm. Recordings are material objects embodying fixations of sounds (excluding, by statutory definition, motion picture soundtracks), such as cassette tapes, CDs, or LPs. Thus, for example, a song (the "work") can be fixed in sheet music ("copies"), in phonograph disks ("recordings"), or both.

Publication

Publication is no longer the key to obtaining a federal copyright as it was under the Copyright Act of 1909. However, publication remains important to copyright owners. Publication is an important concept in the copyright law for several reasons:

- Works that are published in the United States are subject to mandatory deposit with the Library of Congress.

- When a work is published, it may bear a notice of copyright to identify the year of publication and the name of the copyright owner and to inform the public that the work is protected by copyright.

- The use of a copyright notice is no longer required under U.S. law, although it is often beneficial. Use of the notice may be important because it informs the public that the work is protected by copyright, identifies the copyright owner, and shows the year of first publication. Furthermore, in the event that a work is infringed upon, if a proper notice of copyright appears on the published copy or copies to which a defendant in a copyright infringement suit had access, then no weight shall be given to such a defendant's interposition of a defense based on innocent infringement in mitigation of actual or statutory damages, except as provided in section 504(c)(2) of the copyright law. Innocent infringement occurs when the infringer did not realize that the work was protected.

- The use of the copyright notice is the responsibility of the copyright owner and does not require advance permission from, or registration with, the Copyright Office.

Form of Notice for Visually Perceptible Copies

The notice for visually perceptible copies should contain all the following three elements:

- The symbol © (the letter C in a circle), or the word "Copyright" or both; and
- The year of first publication of the work. In the case of compilations or derivative works incorporating previously published material, the year date of first publication of the compilation or derivative work is sufficient. The year date may be omitted where a pictorial, graphic, or sculptural work with accompanying textual matter, if any, is reproduced in or on greeting cards, postcards, stationery, jewelry, dolls, toys, or any useful article.
- The name of the owner of copyright in the work, or an abbreviation by which the name can be recognized, or a generally known alternative designation of the owner. Example: Copyright © 2002 John Doe

The "C in a circle" notice is used only on "visually perceptible copies." Certain kinds of works—for example, musical, dramatic, and literary works—may be fixed, not in "copies," but by means of sound in an audio recording. Since audio recordings such as audio tapes and phonograph disks are "recordings" and not "copies," the "C in a circle" notice is not used to indicate protection of the underlying musical, dramatic, or literary work that is recorded.

The copyright notice should be affixed to copies or recordings in such a way as to "give reasonable notice of the claim of copyright." Example: © 2000 Jane Brown.

The author or copyright owner may wish to place a copyright notice on any unpublished copies or recordings that leave his or her control. Example: Unpublished work © 1999 Jane Doe

Length of Copyright Protection

A work that is created (fixed in tangible form for the first time) on or after January 1, 1978, is automatically protected from the moment of its creation and is ordinarily given a term enduring for the author's life, plus an additional 70 years after the author's death. In the case of "a joint work prepared by two or more authors who did not work for hire," the term lasts for 70 years after the last surviving author's death. For works made for hire, and for anonymous and pseudonymous works (unless the author's identity is revealed in Copyright Office records), the duration of copyright will be 95 years from publication or 120 years from creation, whichever is shorter.

International Copyright Protection

There is no such thing as an "international copyright" that will automatically protect an author's writings throughout the entire world. Protection against unauthorized use in a particular country depends, basically, on the laws of that country.

However, most countries do offer protection to foreign works under certain conditions, and these conditions have been greatly simplified by international copyright treaties and conventions. For further information and a list of countries that maintain copyright relations with the United States, see (Circular 38a) "International Copyright Relations of the United States."

The two major treaties and conventions governing copyright protection internationally are the Berne Convention, and the UCC (Uniform Copyright Convention). Appendix M, at the end of the book, lists the 138 nations that honor one or both of these treaties and conventions. You will notice that most populous countries in the world are listed there as honoring the terms of the Berne Convention or UCC (as of 1998) which nations include about 97% of the estimated world population. That does not mean, however, that the remaining 53 countries will not honor your copyright. Consult your copyright attorney for more details and specific country's policies.

Registration

To register a work, send the following three elements in the same envelope or package to:

Library of Congress
Copyright Office
101 Independence Avenue, S.E.
Washington, D.C. 20559-6000

1) A properly completed application form.
2) A non-refundable filing fee of $30. (NOTE: Copyright Office fees are subject to change. For current fees, please check the Copyright Office Website at www.loc.gov/copyright, write the Copyright Office, or call (202) 707-3000)
3) A non-returnable deposit of the work being registered.

Of course, if your goal is to publish and distribute widely in only one foreign country in addition to the United States, you should consult a good copyright attorney regarding that and all other copyright issues.

Now you can see why copyrighted materials are such a fantastic value in the world of intellectual property—things of value created out of ideas received by your mind. For only $30 each, you can protect the following works in as many countries as you'll visit in your lifetime: Literary, Musical (including words), Dramatic (including music), Pictorial, Graphic, Sculptural, Movies Other Audiovisual Sound Recordings, Architectural

So, all you potential authors and artists out there, get going. You've got the best IP deal going!

Case Study: Winston Churchill

Winston Churchill, the former Prime Minister of Britain, was one of the people most responsible for overcoming the Nazi powers in World War II. I want to focus on his overcoming nature in general, and the way he supplemented his family's income through the discipline of writing.

Winston was born to British high society, being the distant descendant of the Duke of Marlborough and John Churchill. His mother was American, his father a British writer and diplomat. He was a relatively weak and sickly child; and he was bullied by his boarding school classmates. He was challenged by the fact that his parents mostly ignored him, did not visit him at school, and were frequently gone overseas during his holidays. In addition to his great struggle with academics in school, this absence of family contact made his life very difficult.

He finally passed his exams to enter Sandhurst College on his third and final try—his scores did not allow him entrance to Eton—to prepare him for a military career where he ranked only 92 out of 102 (much like Einstein). But, like his father, he found that he enjoyed the freedom of being a war correspondent better—first in Cuba, then India, South Africa, and then Sudan. His style of writing improved, and the British public soon awaited his articles and books describing their empire's latest battles.

Upon Churchill's return to England, he ran for

Minister for Parliament (like our Congress) and was defeated. However, also like his father, he knew that he was called to public life and service in Her Majesty's government. He continued to write to support himself, and his works included popular biographies of his ancestors and his father.

Winston was elected to Parliament on his next try, and served in several successful cabinet posts. He was unfairly blamed for a major mistake as head of the navy in World War I and, as a result, was forced to resign in disgrace and lost his seat in Parliament.

Unsuccessful in his next three bids for Parliament, Churchill was required to depend on his writing income—advances and royalties—for a number of years to support his growing family. Even when he worked in government positions, he needed the extra income that his writing provided in order to make ends meet.

It wasn't until Churchill passed the age of 50 that his writing income began to achieve significant returns. He became known for being paid "a crown per word," and would sometimes leave dinner parties early to trade an extra couple of hours for many pounds.

In addition to the fact that Winston Churchill overcame enormous odds to succeed in politics and life, I have also gleaned the following lessons from his story:

- He followed his good passions and enthusiasm in constantly moving towards that which interested him.

- He kept his day job––politics––and worked additional hours during mornings, evenings, and weekends to continue his writing regimen.
- He read quality books by famous authors and learned how to write well in the process. By doing this, he said that he mastered the art of the English sentence (and it greatly enhanced his vocabulary).
- He learned to adapt his subjects to different markets: first, to those subjects of the British Empire and then to citizens of the United States. Sometimes, two different titles would be chosen for the same book for his two different markets.

Much like Winston Churchill, I believe that writing as a skill can lead to a life in politics. Churchill was predisposed to being elected because his readers appreciated his views, style, and perspective on British politics.

Recommended Reading: Read Jeff Herman's books on how to become a best selling author. He is the founder of The Jeff Herman Literary Agency and has sold hundreds of titles and represents dozens of top authors. My favorite is *You Can Make It BIG Writing Books,* which describes 60 best-selling authors and their experiences, lessons, and lifestyles. Jeff has also written *Writer's Guide to Book Editors, Publishers and Literary Agents,* and *Write the Perfect Book Proposal.* His wife, Deborah Levine Herman, is completing *Writing as a Spiritual Journey.* (Check out one of their books this week.

Recommended Activity: Rent the video, *Finding Forrester* (2000; www.spe.sony.com/movies/findingforrester/), for some important lessons.

"Writers write and readers read" is one of my favorite quotes.

Chapter Eight

Trade Secrets

As we continue our discussion about the different types of intellectual property, we come to the subject of trade secrets. A trade secret is information that companies keep secret to give them an advantage over their competitors. Trade Secrets are good for 100+ years and can cost nothing.

The most famous trade secret in the world is the formulation of Coca-Cola®, which just celebrated its hundredth birthday. Perhaps the second most famous trade secret is how McDonald's makes their French fries taste the way they do. It has something to do with the types of potatoes are grown, where they are grown, and by whom. It probably also has to do with how they are stored, refrigerated, and uniquely processed, and finally, how long they are deep-fried, in what combination of oils, and the secret blend of salts which are used. If you like to eat McDonald's fries along with a Coke (and I am certainly not advocating that for your health, but once in a while it's fun), then you're probably consuming the most powerful combination of trade secrets in the whole world!

Now, let's talk about another secret formulation. Tucked into the gentle rolling hills of southern California is a potter's work shed and kiln. If you were to ask the average person on the street whether money can be made with pottery, most people would answer "not really" or "I don't think so."

The owner of the work shed is a man who just turned 85 years old. Over the years, he perfected a secret formulation for a calming, smooth shade of yellow ceramic glaze, the formula to which he keeps locked in a bank vault. He sells a million dollars worth of this yellow glaze a year to fellow potters! His own pots colored with this glaze routinely sell for $25,000 each, and a major foreign government has offered him a million dollars for the formulation. The formula to that yellow glaze is another example of a trade secret.

Now is the formula for Gatorade® locked in a secret vault somewhere? My sources tell me no. Even though someone could probably reverse-engineer the taste and look of their products (like Powerade® and others), the real value and barrier to new competition entry lies in the brand marketing that they have done, and that they continue to do well. When you spend millions of dollars to define a niche and create brand name equity via a trade name, trademark and tradelook (logo and color scheme), the intellectual property value is more in brand name recognition than the unique formulation itself.

Is the Original Recipe for Kentucky Fried Chicken® in a vault? Yes, evidently it is. For years, Colonel Harland Sanders carried the secret formula for his Kentucky Fried

Chicken in his head and the spice mixture in his car. Today, the recipe is locked away in a safe in Louisville, Kentucky. Only a handful of people knows that particular multi-million dollar recipe, and they've signed strict confidentiality contracts.

The Colonel developed the formula back in the 1930s when he operated a roadside restaurant and motel in Corbin, Kentucky. His blend of 11 herbs and spices developed a loyal following of customers at the Sanders Court & Cafe. "I hand-mixed the spices in those days like mixing cement," the Colonel recalled, "on a specially cleaned concrete floor on my back porch in Corbin. I used a scoop to make a tunnel in the flour and then carefully mixed in the herbs and spices."

Today, the security precautions protecting the recipe would make even James Bond proud: one company blends a formulation that represents only part of the recipe, and another spice company blends the remainder. A computer processing system is used to safeguard and standardize the final blending of the products, but neither company has the complete recipe.

"It boggles the mind just to think of all the procedures and precautions the company takes to protect my recipe," the Colonel said. "Especially when I think how Claudia and I used to operate. She was my packing girl, my warehouse supervisor, my delivery person—you name it. Our garage was the warehouse.

"After I hit the road selling franchises for my chicken, that left Claudia behind to fill the orders for the seasoned flour mix," Colonel Sanders remembered. "She'd fill the day's orders in little paper sacks with cellophane linings and package them for shipment. Then she had to put them on a midnight train." Tittle did the Colonel and Claudia dream in those days that his formula would be famous around the world. I'll talk more more on secret family recipes in the next chapter and franchising in Section IV.

Case Study: Colonel Sanders

It all began with a 65-year-old gentleman who used his $105 Social Security check to start a business. Harland Sanders was born in 1890 in rural Indiana. When he was six years old, his father died, and he had to take care of his younger brother and baby sister. This included learning how to do much of the family cooking. By the age of seven, Harland was a very good cook, accordingly to present-day legend.

When his mother remarried at age 12, he tried a series of jobs to find his niche, which included serving as a soldier in Cuba (he was most likely there when Churchill visited as a new wartime journalist). He tried other occupations, including selling insurance and tires at different points in time, but began to settle on operating gasoline stations.

When he was 40 (about the same age as Ruth Fertel), the Colonel began cooking for hungry travelers who stopped at his service station in Corbin, Kentucky. As more people started coming just for food, he moved across the street to a facility that seated 142. Over the next nine years, he perfected his secret blend of 11 herbs and spices and the basic cooking technique (pressure cooking) that is still used today. As his local and statewide fame grew, the governor made him an honorary Kentucky Colonel, which explains why he began to be known as Colonel Sanders.

But a major setback took place about 15 years later, when he discovered that the new interstate would bypass his town of Corbin. Seeing that the end of his popular restaurant was near, the Colonel auctioned off its assets and paid off his liabilities, and was reduced to living on his $105 monthly government retirement checks once again.

However, being confident of the popularity of his fried chicken, the Colonel devoted himself to the chicken recipe franchising business. He traveled across the country by car from restaurant to restaurant, cooking batches of chicken for their owners and employees. If they loved his recipe, then they would agree to pay him five cents for each chicken that the restaurant would sell. Within 12 years, Colonel Sanders had more than 600 franchised outlets for his chicken in the United States and Canada.

That same year, he sold his ownership interest for two million dollars, and continued as company spokesman until his death. In 12 years, the Colonel went from near-poverty and relative anonymity to having substantial wealth and international fame. Today, over two billion of his "finger lickin' good" chicken dinners are served annually in about 65 countries around the world at over 7000 locations.

Colonel Sanders, a quick service restaurant pioneer, has become a modern day symbol of entrepreneurial spirit, and the world's second most recognizable celebrity.

Draw inspiration from Colonel Sanders. This man, who is yet another example of someone who built a business around an idea, took one thing that he could do well, and created an international business out of it.

Recommended Activity: Rent the movie "What About Bob?" and learn more about "baby steps"—and overcoming the individual fears, weaknesses and obstacles that each of us have, whether we like it or not. We find this movie funny, but it also has a profound practical application for inventors and promising entrepreneurs.

Chapter Nine

Family Recipes

We have now arrived at Family Recipes, which we will discuss separately from trade secrets. Everybody eats, and most everybody has one or more favorite family recipes or they have a friend who does. Investors like to put their money into products or services that people need to have—and food is one of those required things. Food and drink are not only necessities of life, but they can also be fun and signal a celebration of life.

A gentleman from Hawaii began cooking his secret family recipe for pancakes for his friends and an increasing amount of guests. People eventually began to buy his macadamia banana nut creations. He really enjoys what he does, and neither visitors (through word of mouth) nor local residents can get enough of his flapjacks.

We have a Mexican version of KFC here in California called El Pollo Loco™ that features excellent, juicy grilled chicken, tortillas, rice, and beans. When it's properly prepared (some locations are better than others), you take a warm tortilla, put some chicken into it, add some rice, beans and salsa, and it's really delicious and healthy. Evidently, several young men from a poor, northern Mexico village took one mother's recipe for her fruit-based marinade and her cooking technique over a hot, direct fire, and opened several very successful restaurants in southern California. They later sold the small chain to a Fortune 500 corporation for several million dollars. It's not only a true rags to riches story, but it features Hispanic entrepreneurs and highlights the potential value of your family's secret recipe.

Case Study: Famous (Wally) Amos

Today, Wally Amos is an icon in the cookie world and his name is a household word. As founder of Famous Amos Cookies in 1975 and father of the gourmet chocolate chip cookie industry, he has used his fame to support educational causes. Since 1979, Wally Amos has been National Spokesman for Literacy Volunteers of America and is also a Board Member of the National Center for Family Literacy and Communities in Schools. His latest enterprise, The Uncle Noname Company, has been critically acclaimed by the media and consumers alike as a high quality product.

Amos has been the recipient of many honors and awards. He gave the shirt off his back and his battered Panama hat to the Smithsonian Institution's Business Americana Collection. He received an Honorary Doctorate in Education from Johnson & Wales University. He has been inducted into the Babson College Academy of Distinguished Entrepreneurs, and he received the Horatio

Alger Award, The President's Award for Entrepreneurial Excellence, and The National Literacy Honors Award.

He is also an author. He wrote his autobiography, *The Famous Amos Story: The Face That Launched A Thousand Chips,* published by Doubleday in 1983. He collaborated with his son, Gregory, on *The Power In You: Ten Secret Ingredients To Inner Strength,* an inspirational book sharing Wally's philosophy and life experiences, published by Donald I. Fine, in 1988. His book, *Man With No Name: Turn Lemons Into Lemonade,* published by Aslan Press in 1994, tells how he lost everything, including his name but was able to turn adversity into opportunity.

Over the years, Wally has acted in a number of network sitcoms and appeared on hundreds of interview shows and news programs. He is a TV teacher and host of 50 episodes of state-of-the-art programs for adult basic learners that air on PBS stations nationally as part of his strong, ongoing commitment to literary and adult learning. He has acted as product spokesman for several prominent corporations, including Hush Puppies, United Airlines and the California Egg Board.

Famous Wally Amos is now a well-known author and speaker, and popular on the lecture circuit, and encourages others to overcome adversity and give something back to the world. His legacy can be summed up in one quote:

> One person can truly make a difference. If one person has a commitment and belief in their idea, they can succeed. They can overcome anything."

Think back along both sides of your extended family ad try to remember what your family's most famous dish or sauce or recipe is. Do you think it might be good enough to build a business around? Think about it!

Recommended Reading: Top Secret Recipes. This is a fun book and web site by a gentleman named Todd Wilbur (www.topsecretrecipes.com). He gives you recipes for many U.S. restaurants' favorite dishes, many of which began as secret family recipes (and yours is just as good as or even better than theirs!). Buy yours at his web site, www.topsecretrecipes.com or at your favorite bookseller.

Recommend Viewing: The Food Network (www.foodtv. com) is a popular cable television cooking channel that features many restaurants and vendors which began with one great secret family recipe. Their web site gives many excellent, free recipes. Also try Epicurious.com for great meal ideas.

Chapter Ten

Domain (Web Site) Names

I n today's computer savvy world, all of us are probably familiar with the Internet, and those of us who navigate it are familiar with Domain Names. Web site domain names generally follow established (corporate) trademarked names. The University of North Carolina website explains it this way:

> A customer who is unsure about a company's domain name will often guess that the domain name is the company's name. For this reason, "a domain name mirroring a corporate name may be a valuable corporate asset, as it facilitates communication with a customer base." Thus, a domain name is more than a mere Internet address. It also identifies the Internet site to those who reach it, much like a person's name identifies a particular person, or, more relevant to trademark disputes, a company's name identifies a specific company.

The bottom line appears to be that owners of the federal trademark registrations are protected, by the Federal Trademark Dilution Act of 1995 (FTDA) and by the courts, from those who register domain names including the registered marks. This is probably what Congress intended when it passed the FTDA. Senator Leahy made the following statement that has been quoted by almost every court deciding this issue: "It is my hope that this anti-dilution statute can help stem the use of deceptive Internet addresses taken by those who are choosing marks that are associated with the products and reputations of others." (Remarks before the Senate, Dec. 29, 1995, Cong. Rec. S. 19312 [104th Cong. 1995])

There also appears to be an issue of whether the registered trademark is famous. There was a case involving Toys R Us® in which they claimed that 94% of mothers in the United States could readily identify their related businesses which all end in "R Us." So, for most of us whose trademarks are not famous yet, we should consult a trademark attorney if we have a legal question about obtaining or preventing others from using Internet addresses or our trademark. So, if you don't yet have a trademark or a pending application, please go back and review Chapter 6 which deals with trademarks, in order to get one.

As far as international domain name protection goes, search Google under "international domain names." There are some providers that claim to cover 240 different country codes, so if your business is global in nature, check out some of these sites. A good web site consultant can immensely help you in directing traffic to your particular web page. By strategically locating your information on major search engines, you can greatly increase your Internet traffic.

Check out www.register.com and other web sites to help brainstorm what other creative names can be used to achieve the address that you want. They list many available alternative names that may serve your needs. Also, a good web site consultant can cause most search engines to direct inquiries to your site.

Case Study: Ray Bradbury

I love Ray Bradbury's story because I too have children and responsibilities as he did, and I love the idea of writing a rough book draft in nine days!

A science fiction genius, Ray Bradbury "has lived his whole life by these principles:

- Fall in love with one idea after another – and immerse yourself in these loves.
- Follow your heart wherever it leads. Don't ever let anyone talk you out of your dreams. And, in the process, he almost single-handedly created socially-conscious science fiction."

He is passionate about many areas of life and science. "I haven't calmed down since I was 3," he says 74 years later.

Although Bradbury writes constantly, there were times when it was a challenge. Said Bradbury: "I wrote

Fahrenheit 451 in the basement of the UCLA Library; I needed someplace to hide out because I had a house full of children. You rent a typewriter, 10 cents per half-hour, and you type like hell. I spent $9.80, and in 9 days, I had [the first draft of] Fahrenheit 451! I didn't write for kids; I wrote for me——to have fun, to have joy. I never thought it would be in print 47 years."

Write with passion. Find the spark of enthusiasm and don't stop typing. Force your fingers and hands and forearms to get into the steady rhythm of punching out words, phrases, and well-written sentences.

I close with Ray Bradbury's genuine expression of his love for life:

> What is the function of mankind amidst the vast universe? To witness and celebrate! Look upon the Creator, the stunning terror of it all, and celebrate——otherwise, why are we here? Your job is to see, to appreciate – but also to work, improve yourself, improve the world. We represent [Him], and we are beholden to that gift! *——Ray Bradbury*

Recommended Reading: *Leading an Inspired Life,* by Jim Rohn. This book is a compilation of Jim Rohn's lectures on success, with topics ranging from facing your fears to designing your future. This is a must-read book for everyone looking to achieve success by earning it. Jim's philosophy is not a get-rich-quick scheme or getting people to walk on hot coals, but is rather a straightforward instruction book of life.

Section III

The Nuts and Bolts of Running a Business

Chapter Eleven

Forming Your New Business

L et's look at the structure of your business. Say that you have an old, favorite family recipe for preserves, a special dressing, marinade, or condiment. Instead of starting a restaurant around it, or becoming a food supplier or vendor, you have decided to start a gift basket business from your home, using the item as a special attraction. The home-based gift basket business appears to be a good, sideline business for many people. In fact, I saw a survey that said that most established operators make more than $50,000 per year.

First, what do you want to call your business? If your name is Sarah Jane Keller, perhaps you might call it "Sarah Jane's Gift Baskets" or "Sarah Jane's Gifts" or something else. Or, you can begin selling now using your present name, and your customers can simply make out their checks directly to "Sarah Jane Keller." However, if you want your customers to make out their checks to "Sarah Jane's Gift Baskets," then you will want to file what is called a "Fictitious Name Statement" with your county. This will tell local residents that you are Sarah

Jane Keller "Doing Business As" (DBA or d/b/a) Sarah Jane's Gift Baskets.

Your county will generally want you to publish your notice in a local paper for four weeks and then file paperwork with the county records department to that effect. This is to verify that no one objects to your use of that name. This can cost as little as $39.95 and up, depending on prices and services in your county. Generally, the smaller the newspaper, the lower the price.

The next step is to take your proof of DBA to your bank. They will open a business account for you that allows you to deposit and write cheeks using your DBA name. You will still file a personal annual tax return, but you will probably need to attach a Schedule C (Business Expenses) to it. Your tax accountant can help you with the details. A DBA is great to begin with. Even Starbucks uses a DBA—you'll see that in their trademark filings: "DBA Starbucks Coffee Company."

Now, let's say that you get so big that your business attorney and your CPA both encourage you to "incorporate." When you incorporate, you form a new company or corporation as a separate, legal entity. Both your attorney and your CPA can help you to accomplish this, and they can explain the benefits for you when you get to be a certain size. I generally avoid partnerships, because they rarely work out long-term. Some people like limited liability companies/corporations (LLC), and they do have certain advantages. I myself have used them increasingly in recent years.

There are a few more things that you will need to

think about. If you are operating out of your home, then I recommend an insurance rider to your homeowner's policy to adequately protect your family. If you operate at a separate location, then talk with a business insurance specialist. Also, your city may require a business license, and some other permits may be needed by your county or by another regulating body.

Accounting

Now that you have your business underway, you will need monthly or quarterly and annual financial statements, and especially summaries of profit and loss, to monitor your progress and success. In addition to this, you will want to insure the timely payment of payroll, personal, and corporate income taxes.

Say that you've begun selling a few gift baskets, and you are ready for more rapid growth and expansion. If you have a computer, then some popular accounting software programs like Quicken (for simple, home-based businesses) or QuickBooks (for small businesses) may help you immensely in keeping track of income and expenses. That is just another way of saying revenues and costs.

If you have several ladies helping you out of their own homes, at their own pace, and using their own tools and scissors, then you might agree to compensate them on a "piecework" or contract basis. You would pay them per piece of finished product.

The book below, Small Time Operator, will advise you how to choose an accountant to assist you with many of these important details. For example, if your helpers are really employees instead of legal independent contractors, then you are responsible for payroll taxes, which results in a higher level of accounting detail with penalties for non-compliance.

Recommended Reading: *Small Time Operator: How to Start Your Own Business, Keep Your Books, Pay Your Taxes, and Stay Out of Trouble* (25th Edition by Bernard Kamoroff). From the enthusiastic written reviews, its high sales rank (324) and 54 total printings in 22 years (over 500,000 copies sold), most new business owners will find this book useful. It is a great source for understanding the basics of bookkeeping and accounting. The Appendix has a section on how to choose an accountant, Certified Public Accountant (CPA) or Chartered Accountant for your business, which is very important for compilations, counsel and tax preparation.

If that book, along with a popular business accounting software package doesn't satisfy your accounting education needs, then I also recommend *The McGraw-Hill 36-Hour Accounting Course* by Robert Dixon et al, which should sufficiently educate those in charge of the "back office" needs for your business.

Hiring and Managing People

My business strength is financial architecture and one of my major weaknesses is hiring and managing people. Although there are plenty of people who are really good at it, I definitely am not. When you can similarly identify your business strengths and weaknesses, you'll be a better and stronger manager. My best advice for managing people comes from the well-known author and trainer, Ken Blanchard, who coaches many Fortune 500 managers: "Catch people doing something right—and commend them with positive reinforcement." My best advice for hiring people is to start with part-timers to see how they perform before making a commitment to full-time work.

You might want to consider the McDonald's model: locate motivated, franchised hands-on managers; hire and train young people at entry level positions, and keep them busy (Kroc kept them cleaning) when traffic is slow. Considering retired people as part-time help provides a very good maturity balance to the overall mix.

This chapter's recommended reading will help you in your hiring and managing employees.

Case Study: The Coca Cola® Story

In 1886, a pharmacist in Atlanta named John Pemberton was tinkering with medicinal formulas and looking for a solution to headaches. His fragrant, caramel-colored concoction was infused with carbonated water and served to a few drugstore patrons. His bookkeeper named the beverage Coca-Cola and he wrote it out in the script that we still see today.

In its first year, Pemberton sold about nine glasses a day of the innovative drink. That same year, he registered "Coca-Cola syrup and extract" with the U.S. Patent Office.

Unfortunately, he was more of an inventor than

businessperson; four years later, he sold the company to another Atlanta resident for only $2300.

In 1893, the now famous Coca-Cola trademark was filed in the same Patent and Trademark Office. Within two years of that date, the new owner had syrup plants in Chicago, Dallas and Los Angeles, and he could honestly claim that the product was enjoyed in every state in the Union. In fact, the first ten years of Coke's history were a real struggle. Smart and aggressive marketing was what saved the day, and the same is true of most new products. Because of that marketing, over ten billion gallons (similar to McDonald's-type statistics) of that secret syrup have been produced, distributed and sold throughout the world.

A Coke executive was laid over in an Irish airport due to the famous London fog of 1964. He recalled:

> [I] saw a bottle of Coke in a whole new light ... [I] began to see a bottle of Coca Cola as more than a drink that refreshed a hundred million people a day in almost every corner of the globe. So [I] began to see the familiar words, 'Let's have a Coke,' as more than an invitation to pause for refreshment. They were actually a subtle way of saying, 'Let's keep each other company for a little while.' And [I] knew they were being said all over the world as [I] sat there in Ireland.

So that was the basic idea: to see Coke not as it was originally designed to be––a liquid refresher––but as a tiny bit of commonality between all peoples, a universally liked formula that would help to keep them company for a few minutes."

Recommended Reading: *First, Break All the Rules: What the World's Greatest Managers Do Differently* by Marcus Buckingham and Curt Coffman.

Chapter Twelve

Defining Your Niche

One of the most important ways to define your business is to find your niche. Ask yourself, "What makes my business different from my competitors?" Is it quality of service, exclusive patent-pending technology, or something else? What makes your gift basket business different and better than everyone else's? If you can establish yourself in a very unique niche, with your product or service different and better than the others available, then you are not forced to compete solely based on lowest price.

How can you define your customers' problems so that your product or service is the only logical solution? If you are Mrs. Knott (of Knott's Berry Farm fame), and you are serving the best chicken dinners and preserves on the West Coast, then your customers will insist on your solution to their hunger problem. If you are Marie Callender, and you are serving the best pies and homemade soups, then you are the only real solution to your customer's sweet tooth problem. How can you define your business niche so that you are not just another commodity competing on lowest price?

Trying to decide which niche your business is in, it is sometimes hard to do because you are fearful that you will limit your business when you do so. Fear of failure is one of those things that can cause you to lose sight of everything you have worked so hard to get. Making a mistake is not the end of the world for your business. It is better to try out one niche and find that you don't fit rather than trying to be all things to all people and then never find the true outlet for your business.

Overcoming Fear of Failure

Why are we afraid to step out into the unknown? We know that it is certainly in human nature to stay within our comfort zones. I remember an interview with the two founders of Intel. One of them thoroughly enjoyed the journey from the garage to the top of the Fortune 500. The other was scared to death the entire way. Most of us in the United States can relate more to the second co-founder, and this is natural. If you live in Europe or Japan, then you probably have a much greater fear of business failure for very good reasons. Your career can be cut short by a business failure there.

But if we look at most successful people, we see that they have not had unbroken rises to the top. In fact, it pays to beware of unbroken success, because failure is the fertilizer for future success. Most big millionaires failed three times previously, a study showed. It is a fact that we can learn from our mistakes, and there is also a lot of wisdom in learning from other people's mistakes. However, as we learn we must be free to make our own without punishing ourselves afterwards, and without beating ourselves up.

Here's a novel approach to take: "I made a mistake, and I learned a lot from it. I won't make the same mistake again, and I'm better for it. If I hurt you in the process, then I'm sincerely sorry––it was not intentional. I have learned a great deal from my misjudgments, errors, mistakes, and failures."

Another great challenge to stepping out can be a fear of success. We may think: "I don't think that I could handle success. The fame and money would go to my head." I remember scratching my head in disbelief when a friend rejected a promotion because he didn't want the additional headaches. Many people suffer from fear of success. Here's a novel antidote: think of the added influence that you could have with greater success, the greater good that you could do for others, etc.

Dislike of change is another great challenge. We get to a point where we begin to enjoy our comfortable routines, and this makes change. Not necessarily painful, but a stretch.

It is not unusual for bright, creative people to wake up scared about what could go wrong during that day. It's far more common than anyone cares to admit. Since our sub-conscious tends to solve for our most dominant thoughts, it is really important to find a way to overcome these fears.

I like the solution that Mrs. (Debbie) Fields (who found her niche and made the most of it) came up with to overcome these very normal fears:

It's attitude. Whether you think you can or can't—and I'm not saying it's not scary. I'm saying, I wake up saying, "at least I can try," Just like the little train that could, that attitude will get you further and further. At least I can try. The moment you say you can't, you are defeated. You can never use the word can't. You've got to believe. You have to have the right attitude [of courage]. More importantly, you just don't give up.

Case Study: Buckminster Fuller

Buckminster Fuller invented the geodesic dome and a wide range of other paradigm-shifting machines and structural systems. He was especially interested in high strength to-weight designs, with a maximum of utility for minimum of material. His designs and engineering philosophy are part of the foundation of contemporary high-tech design aesthetics.

"'The Dark Ages still reign overall humanity," Fuller wrote in 1932. "We are powerfully imprisoned in these Dark Ages simply by the terms in which we have been conditioned to think." In 1927, Fuller designed the factory-assembled Dymaxion house (making cheap mass produced housing a reality), followed in 1928 by the three wheeled Dymaxion car (technically superior and safer than the .Model T Ford). Fuller's designs encountered resistance from purely profit-driven corporations, whose destructive legacies he would spend the next 50 years fighting.

Throughout the 1940s and 1950s, Fuller gained a

formidable reputation as an early researcher of renewable energy sources. Drawing upon U.S. Navy experiences, Fuller developed tensegrity structures, most notably the Geodesic Dome (minimalist structures that actually get stronger as they get larger). Famous Geodesic Domes include The EPCOT Center at Florida's Walt Disney World and the US Pavilion at the 1967 Montreal World's Fair. Fuller also discovered the science of Synergetics, which explores holistic engineering structures in nature (long before the term synergy became popular).

Fuller's 28 books explore how 100% of humanity could have high living standards (one of my goals also), and have sold over a million copies. Books like Operating Manual for Spaceship Earth (New York: Simon & Schuster, 1969) and Critical Path (New York: St. Martin's Press, 1982) captured a wide audience. These books (and many others) featured systems theory principles, laying the groundwork for authors Alvin Toffler, Toni Peters, John Naisbitt and Peter Senge.

Fuller's efforts were recognized by over fifty honorary degrees in the sciences and humanities, and by his presentation with the Presidential Medal of Freedom from Ronald Reagan in 1981. Though none of his 25 patents achieved spectacular commercial success, he changed the way that the world thinks, and we now routinely expect to help raise living standards around the world over time.

I remember reading that when he viewed magazine racks, say at an airport, he would pick magazines that he knew nothing about, because he recognized the value of cross disciplinary learning. I refer to this approach as "connecting the dots outside the box."

Recommended Reading: *Competitive Strategy* by Michael E. Porter, who was one of our most popular professors at Harvard Business School. The fact that his book sales rank as the 1267th most popular speaks to his broad appeal and readership. Also recommended is *Marketing Outrageously*, by Jon Spoelstra and Mark Cuban is a fun marketing book. In each of the 17 chapters, Spoelstra illustrates one of "ground rules" of marketing, asserting that, for instance, each company must differentiate itself as we have described in this chapter.

Chapter Thirteen

Finding Customers

How are you going to get the word out about your product? You know it's good, but how are you going to convince others that it is? The truth is that it all conies down to good marketing. Innovative, guerrilla (inexpensive) marketing can really make the difference between success and business failure. Listen to Lynne Franks, the lady who promoted Mrs. Field's Cookies in London:

> I launched and promoted Debbie's business 12 years ago, when she came back to the UK. This is one of the most successful aspects of the launch I did for Debbie m London that typifies the sort of creativity new entrepreneurs can easily employ. I sent boxes of hot Mrs. Field's Cookies to all the early morning radio presenters in the areas where Debbie was opening stores, and saw that they were delivered personally just as the broadcasters were about to go on air or when they were already in the studio.

It worked perfectly, was not expensive, and nearly all of the DJs who received them raved about them on the air during their busy morning radio shows. Radio is a very under-appreciated medium. Most stations have high audiences, many of them women, and it's much easier to target your market through radio than it is through television. See if you can persuade your local station to interview you––but don't contact them unless you're sure that your story will work for them. Listen to the show first!"

If you are in the gift basket business, why not do the same thing and send several small baskets and fresh baked goods to some key local radio announcers? Or, if you have access to small, local television stations, you might want to try two-minute advertising spots called "short-form" infomercials.

Another great tool is the Internet. I was watching a television infomercial the other evening, and a lady claimed that she had sold over one million dollars of gourmet gift baskets over the Internet.

Case Study: Abraham Lincoln

Probably the greatest example of persistence is Abraham Lincoln. It you want to learn about somebody who didn't quit, look no further. Born into poverty, Lincoln was laced with defeat throughout his life. He lost eight elections, failed twice in business and suffered a nervous breakdown. He could have quit many times, but he didn't; and therefore he became one of the greatest presidents in the history of America. Lincoln was a champion, and he never gave up.

The following is a sketch (many of you have seen this before, but it bears repeating here) of Lincoln's road to the White House:

1816 His family was forced out of their home.

1818 His mother died.

1831 He failed in business.

1832 Ran for state legislature and lost.

1832 Lost his job and wanted to go to law school, but couldn't get in.

1833 Borrowed some money from a friend to begin a business and by the end of the year he was bankrupt. He spent the next 17 years paying off the debt.

1834 Ran for state legislature again and won.

1835 Was engaged to be married, and his sweetheart died.

1836 Had a nervous breakdown and was in bed for six months.

1838 Sought to become speaker of the state legislature and was defeated

1840 Sought to become elector and was defeated

1843 Ran for Congress and lost

1846 Ran for Congress again––this time he won–– went to Washington and did a good job.

1848 Ran for re-election to Congress and lost

1849   Sought the job of land officer in his home state and was rejected

1854   Ran for Senate of the United States and lost

1856   Sought the Vice Presidential nomination at his party's national convention and got less than 100 votes.

1858   Ran for U.S. Senate again - again he lost

1860   Elected President of the United States of America

Here is what Abraham Lincoln said after one of those defeats: "The path was worn and slippery. My foot slipped from under me, knocking the other out of the way, but I recovered and said to myself, 'It's a slip and not a fall.'" May we recover as gracefully and with his same spirit from our missteps!

Recommended Reading: *Grassroots Marketing: Getting Noticed in a Noisy World* by Shel Horowitz.

Section IV

Building a Business

Chapter Fourteen

The Biography of a Business

As I write this chapter, I am also helping to allocate assets of a particular company in order to help produce three new ventures with fresh vision, staff, and funding. As a way of illustrating the principles and "how to" aspects of this book, I am going to share, in real time, what steps I am taking to launch one of those three new businesses.

The company in question will be a medical device company, with special microscopes that will hopefully be able to automatically detect certain types of cancer from tissue samples. The first thing that I do is to brains
torm with alternative possible names for the venture. I want the name to sound hightech and to clearly brand and identify what solution we are selling. Then, I ask a graphic artist friend to play with looks and logos for the possible names. It helps to make the project more real and viable for me when I look at six possible versions of a company's name. (I'm not saying that should be your first step, but it happens to work very well for me.)

I then look for a part-time Chief Executive Officer. I'm

looking for someone who is prominent and experienced in that business, and fortunately, I happen to know someone who fits that description and is available. My pitch to my potential CEO is that I have a part-time managing opportunity that I would like to sit down and discuss. He is definitely interested, especially when I offer to locate the initial headquarters office as close to his home as is humanly possible. While meeting with my new CEO, I happen to see a sophisticated investor in the same restaurant, and I know that his group is looking for a good, quality biotech/medical device startup to invest in. I also know that his average investment ($575,000) is just what we need for the first year's operation and patent development.

If this deal comes together, then I will offer the CEO 15 percent of the new company, in exchange for quality leadership over the next three years. In a prior deal, we offered ten percent and our prominent friend was satisfied. The investors will get 20 percent of the new company for the first round of funding. The other scientist and technologists will get a good ownership stake also, so everyone will be happy as we get launched.

Here's where the wheels start turning. The CEO, as a part of his job description, will develop the Executive Summary, Marketing and Development Strategy, Business Plan and Investor Presentation. He will set up the new offices and laboratory near his home. The attorneys for the investor will verify that everything is done properly. A fine, local patent firm will develop the new patent applications, which will provide the "exclusive patent pending technologies" that will propel the new company forward. The CEO will build a new management team, including a part-time Chief Financial Officer; begin to build alliances with large business partners; make sure that the working prototype is completed on time and within budget; and handle all of the normal CEO duties.

Those are my real world, day-in-and-day-out action steps for building a new business around intellectual property. For doing this, I would receive five percent of the company and a monthly consulting/advisor's fee for the first several years. That's what my expertise has been in this project: serving as a financial architect. You can do the same, even for your home-based business. It's no different, other than working on a smaller scale.

Case Study: The Ray Kroc Story

Ray Kroc was born in 1902 in Oak Park, Illinois. At the age of 20, he landed a job as a salesman for the Lily Tulip Cup Company. In the course of selling paper cups, Ray met Earl Prince, who had invented a five spindle multimixer for making milk shakes, and who was also buying Lily cups by the truck load.

Fascinated by the speed and efficiency of Earl's machine, Kroc obtained rights to sell it. On his sales travels, he heard about a remarkable restaurant in San Bernardino, California, owned by two brothers, Dick and Mac McDonald, who had purchased eight of these multimixers and had them churning out milkshakes all day long. At the age of 52, Ray sold the brothers on the idea of opening several more McDonald's outlets under his management.

Kroc commented, "I was 52 years old. I had diabetes and incipient arthritis. I had lost my gall bladder and most of my thyroid gland in [World War II] campaigns, but I was convinced that the best was ahead of me." His convictions about his destiny, and the future of McDonald's, eventually convinced the brothers to sell out to him in 1961 for only $2.7 million. In less than three years after being introducing as the famous clown, Ray Kroc's Ronald McDonald was recognized by 96% of American children!

Like Walt Disney, Ray Kroc was a stickler for cleanliness. One of his favorite sayings was "If you have time to lean, then you have time to clean." Next time you visit one of his restaurants, you'll notice the young staff continuously cleaning the whole facility.

Although Kroc succeeded in adapting a local fast-food concept to the changing tastes of American families and taking it around the world. His formula of clean facility, friendly service, low prices, no waiting, and no reservations, helped to change and serve the modern world.

Chapter Fifteen

Building a Business
Around a Patent

This chapter is for all you inventers who have taken the first step and begun your business by filing a patent. After you've filed your Formal Patent Application or Provisional Patent Application, the next and most important step (and the one ignored by most inventive people) is to develop a plan for making money using the pending patent. In other words, you need to decide how you are going to commercialize your innovation. What is the most efficient way to bring this product or service to market? Normally, this initial strategic thinking will be going on simultaneously with your trip to the patent attorney and gives you the needed encouragement to move forward on all fronts: obtaining the patent, making your business and marketing plans, raising money, and recruiting key people.

The process of thinking through the nature and organization of the business is vital, and it should eventually result in a written, typed business plan of about 20 pages.

There are some good, reasonable software packages that can help you immensely with this process. The summary of your business plan—the part that prefaces it—is called the Executive Summary and consists of 3 pages.

When preparing your presentations, you should bear in mind that less is definitely more. Watching television and living fast-paced lives have shortened everyone's attention span—even that of those who may be scanning (scanning is a more accurate word here than reviewing) your documents and who may want to fund your deal. Bearing this in mind, you should make the most of the time that they give you. Your Executive Summary and your Investor Presentation will need to be brief and crisp. Bounce your business idea off positive friends and associates first, using these documents, and they will probably make good suggestions and ask you probing questions that demand convincing, businesslike answers. Those answers should then be incorporated in your summary and presentation.

It's possible to start a business on just one good idea, and it's been done repeatedly by many successful businesses such as Kodak, Polaroid, Xerox, Intel and other large companies. Many of these companies then go on to develop further inventions and products that multiply the number of their successful patents and help them build their company even stronger.

The following are three different viable businesses that I have worked with in the past—all promising, with great potential. Let me describe some of these real-world situations to you.

- A biotech company has 15 different pieces of intellectual property (patents pending, licenses, options to license, new patents to file), which taken together is called a "patent portfolio" or an "intellectual property portfolio." Their original patent application, still pending, is important, but it is another, more recent, patent application that larger pharmaceutical companies are most interested in for potential commercial uses. Four million dollars have been raised from investors and spent so far, and the company's future seems to hinge more on obtaining, perfecting and expanding the commercial value of this second, more valuable patent than the one they initially had.

- A particular mass merchandiser successfully marketed an engine oil treatment as the "only patented product of its kind," and it has sold over $100 million worth of the product to date. Thus far, investors have put over five million dollars into this company and its products, and the patent still has five more years of "protection" left.

- A venture-capital backed energy company used a highly regarded, regional patent law firm to file a large initial patent application on a particular discovery that has broad uses for fossil fuels. After raising another million dollars from investors and working further on the patent, it was decided to split up the larger application into as many as ten smaller and narrower––and probably more easily approved––patent applications.

Each one of the above companies have used one or more patents on which to base their solvency. Many smart investors today expect a new business to have at least one solid, quality pending patent application on file in Washington, D.C. in order to qualify as a viable company in which to invest. The patent makes it harder for competitors to make a profit from your ideas. Of course, successfully issued patents do not guarantee commercial rewards, but they do increase your chances dramatically of achieving and maintaining marketplace success.

Prototypes

Prototypes are essential to capitalizing on your patent. A prototype is nothing more than a working model of what you are trying to raise funds to produce. Depending on what type of idea or invention you are trying to sell, your prototypes will take different forms.

For the inventor, the prototype is a summary of the invention that contains diagrams or better yet, a working model of your product. For the entrepreneur trying to build a business, it is coming up with enough concrete figures to convince investors that, the idea has taken shape and will progress into the marketplace.

For the biotech company mentioned earlier, the prototype was a demonstration to the potential investor of the "world's smallest and thinnest needle," which was the subject of the patent attorney's work on the first patent application. It was tangible, it worked under a microscope, and it represented the successful completion of months of experimentation.

For the consumer products company, the working prototype consisted of bottles of specially formulated chemicals that could be reliably demonstrated on a portable test machine, which had a pending patent application and had already sold approximately $600,000 over the prior 12 months—proving customer acceptance.

For the energy company, the working prototype consisted of volumes of credible test results, conducted by reputable laboratories, two existing patents, prior commercial success, and a good business plan.

For a new pet product invention developed by a friend of mine, a working prototype took only several hours to develop. It was made from a few cent's worth of cardboard and demonstrated that the concept worked on his dog.

For a new Dairy Queen type concept by that same friend, a working prototype would probably cost him and his friends about $300,000. However, there was an easier solution to his problem. Since his idea consisted of raking a successful food product from another part of the United States to his region, he was able to easily use the successful existing operations as examples of his working prototypes and save the initial expense. This is one advantage of a franchised or licensed business opportunity as described further later in this section—especially when it comes to a restaurant or other retail food preparation business.

For a computer software company, a working

prototype consisted of getting a prominent county government to install and use its patent-pending (for design) and copyrighted (for unique coded) software.

You can see that there are nearly as many prototypes as there are ideas and inventions, so it's up to you to decide which will work best for you.

Checklist: "Protecting your idea while you work to take it to market"

1) Have you visited a patent attorney? Can you at least claim "patent-pending" protection for your invention and ideas?

2) Have you begun on your Executive Summary yet? Read through the appendix and visualize how you would adapt your business idea to that format.

3) Do you have talented and trusted business, legal, and accounting advisors with whom you can meet with and brainstorm to get started?

4) How will you bring your idea to the marketplace? In what form and at what price will it be produced? What is your proposed business model or revenue model?

5) How long will it take to produce a working prototype? How much will it cost?

6) Do you already have some ideas of who can serve part-time in some of your key organizational positions (more on this in a later chapter)?

7) What will you need in order to create a rough draft of a Business Plan and Investor Presentation?

Virtually every day of a normal week, my clients' discussion of their business activities includes conversations regarding patent-related issues. One used to think about just one major patent per business, but technology advancements have recently caused high-tech professionals to begin talking about "a bundle" oi patents surrounding a particular type of technology. This is now referred to as "a patent portfolio or estate," "intellectual property portfolio," "IP portfolio," or just IP.

We discussed this earlier as including trademarks, trade secrets, copyrights. These days, I am hearing more and more references to IP, or intellectual property, when they specifically mean patents, so be ready if and when someone brings up the question, "What is the status of your IP?" What they want to know is it you have a good, solid patent pending in Washington, D.C. for your "exclusive patented (or patent pending) technology." We will show you, in Chapter 12, how to answer that question in the affirmative for very little upfront money.

Case Study: Thomas Alva Edison

Thomas Edison, the prolific American inventor, is best known for inventing the light bulb, the phonograph, and the forerunner of the VCR/TV. He also made major improvements to existing prototypes of the stock ticker, telegraph, and telephone. His expertise was concentrated on devices that could utilize electricity, and which forever changed our culture and the world's lifestyle. The following are a few specific lessons we can learn from this great inventer:

1. Turning ideas into commercially useful products, items or services is a life-long process––not a one time event. It's a journey of discovery rather than a temporary stopping point. Being faithful to your first idea is critical to handling the second one even better. Being open continually to new, improved, outside-the-box ways to accomplish something, solve a problem, or meet a pressing need is what will bring you success.

2. It is very hard to know, in advance, which invention will be successful. Many times, discovery happens as an accidental byproduct of other research and pursuing other ideas. As great an invention as the incandescent light bulb eventually turned out to be, if the economics of production hadn't turned out to be relatively low and well accepted by the public, we might still be using candles today. Those particular economics and market conditions are generally beyond an inventor's control, but must be taken into consideration.

3. You can expect opposition and adversity. Edison was in constant litigation, defending his patents, for the rest of his life.

4. Hard work is obviously important to idea success. Over the past hundred years, a newer model has emerged for "idea" people. Whereas Edison cited only 1% inspiration and frequent 20-hour days

(99% hard work), other idea friends and I agree that now it can he "50% daily inspiration, and 50% follow through."

Dr. Cho, of Korea, who built an idea into the world's largest church, explains his secret this way: "[Each day] I pray and I obey." Good food for thought. In any case, I trust that you will do something soon with your unique idea.

Recommended Reading: Dr. John Gray's materials; especially *Men are front Mars, Women are from Venus*. There is a very good reason why he has sold over 13 million copies of this book and series. For all you authors out there, Dr. Gray self-published his first several books to get going. Then, after attracting enough attention in New York City (the publishing center of the United States) to land a major publisher, he conceived of the need for this concept and wrote the series of books––and the rest is history.

Do yourself a favor and take a serious look at these books. And remember, without your understanding of your spouse or significant other and their support of you––you will be at a major disadvantage in developing inventions and ideas!

Chapter Sixteen

Raising Money
For Your New Business

The part of the process of starting a business venture that can be the most intimidating to many people is raising money. As Jason McCabe Calacanis, Editor and CEO of *Venture [Capital] Reporter* stated: "Perhaps one of the hardest things for an entrepreneur today is to raise a first round of capital." Sure, your idea is good, and you believe in it, but how can you get others to believe in it enough to invest in it since the financial risk is the highest for investors at the beginning of a deal because there are many things that frequently can and do go wrong at that stage of the game.

The following is Jason Calacanis' solution:

> If you want to raise money for your company, the best thing that you can do right now is to find a serial entrepreneur––one who has sold or taken a company public––and make him or her your CEO. Don't be tied to the title of CEO. Instead,

leverage someone else's track record, and enjoy the title of Chairman or President.

The word "serial," as Jason uses it here, means, "repeat." He is describing an entrepreneur who repeatedly begins and builds successful companies. It is extremely helpful to have someone like this to finance and run the daily details of your startup and to allow you to be the visionary you need be. This set-up also gives you the time to look at the bigger picture and continue to invent other new things. Hopefully your serial entrepreneur will be able to handle the financial end of the things so you won't have to sweat the payroll unless you are equipped to do so. I have managed to escape weekly payroll headaches for many years, and I am happier and healthier for doing so. Let the serial entrepreneur have the headaches, and you can enjoy the title and function of Chairman or President. It couldn't be sweeter for you.

Angel Groups

Okay, so you need a serial entrepreneur, but how do you locate and recruit such a person? Most metropolitan areas of the United States have several "angel" groups (see the appendix for ¡note information). Angels are seasoned, experienced entrepreneurs, and executives who have been successful in the past, and who are looking for quality new ventures on which to spend their time and money. They can literally be "God's helpers," as their name implies. Get to know several members of these angel groups and ask for their advice.

Dr. Peter Drucker, the famous business author, says that it normally takes three years to build a seasoned, quality, strong management team that has members who are all motivated in the same direction. Through the successful use of angels, advisors, and an experienced CEO, you can substantially speed up this process by forming a seasoned team with each full or part-time employee that you hire. In other words, a part-time local CEO may have a CEO that he or she has worked with previously and successfully; that CEO may have a favorite bookkeeper and outside CPA firm that she or he has worked well with before, and so on.

Let one of these angels review and suggest improvements to your short Executive Summary. Let your new CEO perfect the Executive Summary, Business Plan and Investor Presentation from his or her experience in raising monies previously, and then work together on a series of investor presentation appointments to get vital feedback and to help "perfect the pitch." Sophisticated investors and entrepreneurs talk about the need for an "elevator pitch"—a 30 second "sound bite" that you would use on a stranger during a short elevator ride.

For those desiring to start a home-based business such as the single mother wanting to start a gift-basket or other food business, I won't bore you here with the specific concepts involved in developing business plans to grow a $100 million corporation. If you do require a business plan, though, be sure to follow the formats and include the concepts and terms listed in the Appendix to insure maximum success.

Some investors are constantly looking for the next great thing, so if you believe that you have it, then convince them with conventional, proven, smart investor materials described in this book, and work out mutually agreeable terms.

The process can also be described as: "revise, then test; revise, then test." Revise your presentation and sweeten your offering to be more attractive, and then test it on some new prospects. Then repeat as many times as needed until you have it perfected. When two out of three potential investors nod their heads in warm approval, then you will know you are close to your funding. (As I wrote this book, many smaller companies were paying 20% effective annual rates of return to attract risk capital, while financial institutions were offering consumers only 1.5%!)

Case Study: Andrew Carnegie

If you study the details of the life of Andrew Carnegie, you will find a man who was famous for his ability to produce millionaires. In fact, 43 people from among his own employees became millionaires! Carnegie knew how to bring about change in people. He helped them realize their hidden treasure within, inspired them to develop it, and then watched with encouragement as their lives became transformed.

That is what I want to help you to accomplish. I want you to take small, achievable steps each week, if possible, in order to realize the hidden treasure inside of you and to help inspire you to develop your talent and ideas. I have helped a number of individuals to achieve millionaire status over the past decade. Some have said that I have "birthed many millionaires," and if some of you readers achieve that level of stewardship, then I have a shot at breaking Carnegie's record. But, becoming a millionaire is only a one dimensional measurement of personal achievement––much like grades or SAT scores––and I'm not advocating that pursuit, nor am I bragging. I simply want to encourage each of you to become all that God has destined for you to be; and, if God chooses to make you a millionaire, please have it certified by an accountant and send me a copy so I can rejoice with you.

The psychologist William James once said, "Compared to what we ought to be, we are only half awake. We are making use of only a small part of our physical and mental resources. [Each of us] lives tar within his [or her] limits." In other words, we are living way beneath our potential. We have only developed a small percentage of our abilities, so let's use more, say, 25% to 50%––little by little.

Recommended Reading: Read several of Dr. Peter Drucker's best-selling books on the management of the corporation and organization. I had the rare privilege of studying with Dr. Drucker at the Claremont School of Business. He has an amazing ability to look back over the last 300 years and identify seismic shifts in business trends.

His five most popular books are *The Essential Drucker, Management Challenges, Post-Capitalist Society, The Effective Executive,* and *Innovation and Entrepreneurship.* The last one is my personal favorite. Check out his quotes and list of available books today at www.corpedia.com/welcome/peterdrucker.asp or www.josseybass.com or at booksellers everywhere.

Chapter Seventeen

Building Your New Organization

I n the last chapter, we talked about recruiting a team to help you attract potential investors. A competent and talented management team can be one of the biggest attractions to a potential investor. You will need to carefully choose members of the team based on their expertise and proven track record.

As you work on your Executive Summary and Business Plan, your potential investors will be looking closely at the structure of your team. The hierarchical structure of the team will look something like this (this is also called an organization chart):

Shareholders   SCORE (initially)
                    Chairman and President: You
Directors   Advisors
                    Chief Executive Officer (CEO)
                    Your new full- or part-time recruit

Chief Tech. Officer   Chief Market. Off.   Chief Fin. Off.
     (CTO)   (CMO)   (CFO)

Let's talk about each of these standard positions, which your angel and other advisors and CEO can help you to till:

Shareholders––each person who pays for or earns "shares" in your company is called a shareholder. One share of common stock is a tiny piece of ownership in your new company. As a group and individually, your shareholders have various legal rights, depending on the stare in which you operate. Normally, these shareholders meet once a year to help elect the directors of your Company and to vote on other key issues.

Directors––these are generally experienced businesspeople that have learned how to run, manage, and govern a corporation. You will probably begin with three directors and expand to five and then seven as you grow. It is wise to have a certain minority number as "outside" directors––that is, they do not receive a paycheck as an employee or officer that would make them "insiders." Ratios of one out of three, two out of five, or three out of seven are normal, and this gives investors confidence that both compensation and financial statements are fairly computed. The directors approve the choice of CEO because it is a very important decision. In addition, the board is responsible for keeping the CEO focused strategically and keeping the company well financed.

Chairman––each year, the board of directors, as a group, elects someone to serve as Chairman of the Board. You may also have someone prominent serve as Vice-Chairman, which adds credibility. Sometimes, it is to an inventor's or founder's advantage to get kicked up to Chairman Emeritus status, which provides honor and compensation, but still allows you more free time to pursue other ideas with rich potential. The Chairman guides each Board of Directors meeting.

Advisors—smart companies have at least two or three very talented business advisors who can serve on a Board of Advisors. Since this advisory board does not have the legal liability of the governing and controlling Board of Directors, it is generally easier to recruit experienced businesspeople to this function. These advisors advise the Chairman, the Board, the President and the CEO. One company that I have helped has three advisors, each of whom receives 50,000 warrants per year for their time. One of those advisors is a talented, local angel; another is a member of a prominent consulting firm; and the third is a very successful headhunter (executive search consultant).

CEO—The Chief Executive Officer should be a dynamic, never ceasing source of energy and charisma—a make-it-happen kind of person. Many times, the ideal CEO is a repeat entrepreneur who has had several business successes before. He or she raises money, makes business development deals benefiting the company, and meets with the largest potential customers and vendors to sell them on working with your particular firm.

CTO--the Chief Technical Officer is normally the senior scientist or engineer who knows the most about your invention and technology.

CMO--the Chief Marketing Officer used to be known as the Vice President of Marketing, but times and titles are changing. This person is responsible for all the marketing and selling activities of your company. The entire company should be oriented towards your customers, but the CMO must constantly be focused on these specific duties.

CFO--the Chief Financial Officer is responsible for being steward of all of the finances and assets of the Company. He or she typically has someone assisting; like a controller or head/chief accountant, who actually keeps track of each transaction and summarizes them monthly in Financial Statements (see Appendix I).

Free Advisors--Service Core of Retired Executives (SCORE). The U.S. Department of Commerce sponsors an excellent free service called SCORE. These retired executives have tremendous accumulated wisdom and contacts that are invaluable to your new enterprise. More than 900 business volunteers from around the country donate their expertise as email counselors to help today's entrepreneurs achieve their dreams. SCORE'S team of virtual volunteers can help your small business grow and thrive. Get free and confidential email counseling today by contacting your local SCORE office as listed geographically in Appendix G.

One thing to keep in mind while assembling your team is that you can literally "rent" a talented person for any one or more of these positions. For example, some companies may rent a prominent CEO or experienced CFO in exchange for stock, options, warrants and/or some other agreed-upon compensation when your company is properly funded.

Checklist:

1) Have you contacted SCORE toll-free yet at 800-634-0245 to set up an appointment?
2) Have you considered filling some positions with part-time experts or successful retirees or "in-betweeners"?

Case Study: Benjamin Franklin

Benjamin Franklin was the first famous inventor in the United States; as well as a prominent diplomat and civic leader. He invented bifocals, the flexible urinary catheter, watertight bulkheads for ships, the lightning rod, the first odometer (for horse-drawn carriages), and many other devices that helped people live better and safer and more comfortable.

One of my favorite quotes from Benjamin Franklin is this: "Well done is better than well said." We should appreciate this advice, particularly coming from another inventor, because he knew that action is so much better than mere words. Intent followed by words is a big step, but the next tangible step of moving words into action is the most important because it creates energy, momentum, and a path on which to run. Ben Franklin was definitely a person of action.

Personal need is a powerful force that spurs innovation. Franklin had poor distance vision and also needed glasses to read. He became tired of constantly taking one pair off and putting the other on, so he decided to figure out a way to make one pair of glasses let him see both near and far objects. He cut two pairs of spectacles in half and put half of each lens in a single frame. Franklin's need and innovation led to a solution to his problem.

The needs of our friends are also powerful forces to motivate creativity. Franklin's older brother suffered front kidney stones, and the inventor wanted to alleviate his discomfort. In addition, he had a genuine interest in how the human body works, so, he invented a medical device for him––the first of its kind in the United States.

We should make the most of our experiences. Franklin's diplomatic duties caused him to make eight voyages across the Atlantic Ocean. These were long journeys, and his natural curiosity caused him to investigate a way to make ships work better and more safely. If we keep our eyes open in the same way, we can learn to keep the idea process working at all times.

Businesses can be built around new discoveries. From his development of the furnace stove, Franklin went on to form the first fire company and the first fire insurance company, in order to help people live more safely.

You can be a writer/editor, business and civic leader, or an idea person––all of these are available to you, just as they were to Benjamin Franklin who combined all three professions. Take a minute and think how you might accomplish any or all of them or perhaps other positions better suited to you.

Recommended Activity: Fog onto www.score.org right now to see what free services and articles they can offer you—including a new email counseling service. If you can meet with an expert counselor in person, then please take advantage of the opportunity.

It was this no-cost step that proved to be a major breakthrough for an inventor friend of ours and another client as well. Just that one SCORE counselor helped to create a total of about $60 million in market capitalization and growth. I trust that it will be helpful for you too when you are ready to seriously move ahead with bringing your idea to market.

Chapter Eighteen

Bringing in Investors

L et's first discuss the issue oi debt versus equity. From years of experience, the advice I always give is to avoid debt as much as possible (which always becomes your sole responsibility via personal guarantees), and let other people share your risks in the form of equity.

A proven wav to raise money is by engaging the services of someone whose gifting and expertise is raising money for companies. Assuming that they have a good track record, let them sell small pieces of your company's equity in the form of common shares. These small pieces are called "stocks" or "securities." Your business attorney can recommend a good securities attorney who can keep you legal and recommend some proven fundraisers to meet with and interview.

It seems to everyone at first that one major investor is easier to obtain and more efficient to maintain, but that is a deceptive mirage: most larger investors have large egos, expect you to do what they dictate, and want to control you and your deal. If they don't get 51% on the first round, then they'll want it by the close of the second.

Therefore, assume that you'll seek broader investor representation. The first check is the hardest to get because no one likes to be the first cash investor. You'll find that it will be easier to build momentum and confidence after receiving the first several checks.

The terms that you offer to 10-25 investors should be substantially the same. I've seen the number of warrants (stock options) vary as a "sweetener." If you improve the offering, then go back and make it retroactive to the first several investors also. That's only fair, and it shows good integrity as management.

Case Study: The North Carolina Hair Care Man

We all know that the road to achievement can be slow and difficult, but the Joe Dudley story is proof that dedication, hard work, and persistence does lead to success. It all began when Joe L. Dudley, Sr. invested $10 in a Fuller Products Sales Kit in 1957 and began the challenge of door-to-door selling in Brooklyn, New York. Together with his wife, also a Fuller Products salesperson, he began working with S.B. Fuller, one of the giants in African-American entrepreneurship, and one of the first millionaires.

In 1967, the Dudleys opened a distributorship in Greensboro, North Carolina. As their client base increased, there came a point when Fuller was unable to supply them with all the products they needed for their customers. This forced them to venture into the product manufacturing area. Initially, the products were made in their home kitchen, where Mrs. Dudley and the children would package them at night for Joe and his sales force to deliver the next day. They began to expand their "Dudley Scalp Special" branded product line on a shoestring budget.

By 1976, the Dudley's sales force had grown to 400 strong, and they developed their company policy to only sell to licensed hair and cosmetics professionals. In spite of that limitation (not selling retail), Dudley Products became a multimillion-dollar hair care enterprise. In 1986, their continued growth allowed them to move into a new 37,000 square foot Corporate Headquarters building; and eight years later, they moved into an 80,000 square foot state of the art facility in Kemersville, North Carolina. Their growth continued internationally also, with programs for Zimbabwe, South Africa, Brazil and the Caribbean nations.

A recipient of the Horatio Alger Award, Joe Dudley and his family are committed to see people succeed and realize "The American Dream." Joe Dudley says that happiness is not measured in material success, but by giving back something to make life better for others, and he has created a number of innovative programs for youth and communities.

Recommended Reading: *The Millionaire Next Door* is taken from a real, in-depth study of how millionaires in the United States actually live––and not as the media portray them. I can honestly say that you will be very surprised at what the authors discovered.

Chapter Nineteen

Franchising

We discussed in an earlier chapter how Colonel Harland Sanders became successful by selling franchises of his business. Franchising is a system for operating a specific type of business that includes the rights to use a franchisor's trademarked name and logo and copyrighted systems manual(s) for operating the franchisee's business.

Franchisees––those who purchase and operate a franchise––benefit from proven methods of operation and revenue models. One can compare monthly, quarterly and annual results against those of other franchisees for ideas of improving profitability. Good franchisors provide centralized schooling and training, regional trainers and coaches, and proven troubleshooters to help you if you get into serious trouble. Franchisees can also benefit from local, regional and national advertising cooperative programs.

Take a quick look at the following website to see Entrepreneur.com's annual listing of Entrepreneur's Franchise 500 for 2003.: www.entrepreneur.com/

Franchise_Zone/FZ_Special_Listing/1,4731,12-12–—F5-,00.html

The top ten franchises for 2003 are:

- Subway (for the tenth time)
- Curves for Women (30-minute weight & fitness centers)
- 7-Eleven Inc. (convenience stores)
- McDonald's (fast food locations)
- Jani-King (commercial cleaning)
- Taco Bell Corp
- Quizno's Franchise Co. (sub sandwiches and more)
- Super 8 Motels, Inc.
- Jackson Hewitt fax Service
- Sonic Drive-In Restaurants

Their lowest cost (low end of the range) for HIome-Based franchises are:

2002 Rank	Franchisor	Invest. Amt.
1	Jani-King	$8200
4	CleanNet	3900
5	Jazzercise	1800
8	Coverall	6300
10	Jan-Pro	1000
14	Candy Bouquet	7300

Let's say that you decide, after much research, that you want to purchase a Jan-Pro franchise for your city for $1000. Federal and state rules require the franchisor to disclose the average incomes of their franchisees, and many other details through a Uniform franchise Offering Circular. You may determine that it's a good business for you and your family, and that the likelihood of good returns on investment is high. Perhaps an investment of several thousand dollars would bring your extended family over $50,000 per year in potential projected income. So, you can see that, for the right people, franchises can be the right way to go into business for themselves.

Case Study: The Value of Sales Training

While in college, I was reviewing my course load and limited job experience with one of my Harvard Business School professors and his assistant. He turned to his assistant and they both shook their heads in agreement. "You need some real-world sales training," they said. So, that summer, I was ringing doorbells in Boston, knocking on people's doors and trying to sell them Electrolux vacuum cleaners. It was hot, muggy, and the most valuable experience that I will never forget.

Many people may feel that they could never sell anything, but the fact is that we are always selling ourselves, our ideas, or convincing others to help us get through our "to do" list. But most of the time we don't realize that we are selling. One only has to look at some of the lives of our inventors and business innovators we have already studied to grasp the importance of sales training:

- Harland Sanders (who was awarded his Kentucky Colonelship later) first learned to sell tires, insurance, gasoline and food. After he devised his famous recipe, he had to convince 600 separate franchisees to make it, sell it to their own customers, and pay him a nickel per chicken served.

- Ray Kroc learned to sell paper cups, and then multimixers, and then he had to sell his potential to the McDonald brothers. Eater, he sold his franchisees, and then the American public, and then the world. When you understand how difficult it can be to make a sale, then you appreciate how special something is that sells well such as the Krispy Kreme doughnuts.

- Joe Dudley and his wife first learned how to sell Fuller Products before they could sell their own Dudley Products.

- Mary Kay, Rich DeVos, Zig Ziglar and so many others got their start by learning the secrets of how to sell products to consumers.

We often joke about how someone can sell ice to an Eskimo, meaning that they can convince someone to buy something that they don't need. However, selling with integrity and sincerity of purpose is better. If we really believe in the product or service that we represent, we can do it with a clear conscience.

For my part, I can naturally convey to others: my enthusiasm for Motorola i-1000 plus cellphones (great proven durability plus wonderful speakerphone capabilities); Toyota vehicles (excellent R&D budget and reliable cars and trucks); and free business cards from VistaPrint.com (credit to Matt Davenport and Rhonda Reardon for this find—250 quality cards free plus choose the expedited shipping option for $8).

I could not market most fast food (although Taco Bell has some innovative, healthier items), whole-life insurance, or STP gas and oil products, because I personally don't believe in their general benefits. (Hopefully, I didn't just gore your sacred cow, but forgive me if I did). Genuine, well-founded enthusiasm and sincerity of purpose makes for a natural selling process. I could base sold Electrolux vacuum cleaners because I believed that they were the best product available at the time.

Recommended Reading: Entrepreneur Magazine's Annual Top 500 Franchise Issue, at www. entrepreneurmagazine.com

Section V

Some Last Words...

Chapter Twenty

Preparing to Get Started

Nothing new will happen in your life until you begin to move in a new direction. I commend you for reading this book as your first step forward, and now I recommend that you take your next important step. Albert Einstein said, "Nothing happens until something moves," and this is not only a law of physics, but also of life and business.

A recent, new development in the field of physics actually says, "If you expect to see a particle, then you will. But you will not see it if you are not expecting to see it!" So, in a similar vein, I say to you, "If you expect to receive a new idea and receive a new way of accomplishing something, then you will!" I receive too many emails and verbal confirmations of this truth to tell you otherwise.

If you have not already done, so, then one day soon you will receive a "mother lode" idea. Then, it will be time to pull out this book and review again the many ways and steps that you can take to develop your new idea. You will find that, as you take those baby steps, you will then begin to receive even more new ideas!

Case Study: Madam C.J. Walker

Madame C.J. Walker was born born Sarah Breedlove on December 23, 1867 on a Delta, Louisiana plantation. The Madam C.J. Walker website at www.madamecjwalker. com recounts part of her own story:

"I am a woman who came from the cotton fields of the South. From there I was promoted to the washtub. From there I was promoted to the cook kitchen. And from there I promoted myself into the business of manufacturing hair goods and preparations...I have built my own factory on my own ground" (July, 1912)

...this daughter of former slaves transformed herself from an uneducated farm laborer and laundress into of the twentieth century's most successful, self-made women entrepreneur. Orphaned at age seven, she often said, "I got my start by giving myself a start."

Sarah and her older sister, Louvenia, survived by working in the cotton fields of Delta and nearby Vicksburg, Mississippi. At age 14, she married Moses McWilliams to escape abuse from her cruel brother-in-law, Jesse Powell. When her husband died two years later, she moved to St. Louis with her daughter to join her four brothers who had established themselves as barbers. Working for as little as $1.50 a day, she managed to save enough money to educate her daughter. Friendships with other black women who were members of St. Paul A.M.E. Church and the National Association of Colored Women exposed her to a new way of viewing the world.

During the 1890s, Sarah began to suffer from a scalp ailment that caused her to lose most of her hair. She experimented with many homemade remedies and store-bought products, including those made by Annie Malone, another black woman entrepreneur. In 1905, Sarah moved to Denver as a sales agent for Malone, then married her third husband, Charles Joseph Walker, a St. Louis newspaperman. After changing her name to "Madam" C.J. Walker, she founded her own business and began selling Madam Walker's Wonderful Hair Grower, a scalp conditioning and healing formula, which she claimed had been revealed to her in a dream.

To promote her products, the new "Madam C.J. Walker" traveled for a year and a half on a dizzying crusade throughout the heavily black South and Southeast, selling her products door to door, demonstrating her scalp treatments in churches and lodges, and devising sales and marketing strategies. In 1908, she temporarily moved her base to Pittsburgh where she opened Lelia College to train Walker "hair culturists." By early 1910, she had settled in Indianapolis, then the nation's largest inland manufacturing center, where she built a factory, hair and manicure salon and another training school.

As her business continued to grow, Walker organized her agents into local and state clubs. Her Madam C.J. Walker Hair Culturists Union of America convention in Philadelphia in 1917 must have been one of the first national meetings of businesswomen in the country. Walker used the gathering, not only to reward her agents for their business success, but to encourage their political activism as well. "This is the greatest country under the sun," she told them. "But we must not let our love of country, our patriotic loyalty cause us to abate one whit in our protest against wrong and injustice. We should protest until the American sense of justice is so aroused that such affairs as the East St. Louis riot be forever impossible."

By the time she died at her estate, Villa Lewaro, in Irvington-on-Hudson, New York, she had helped create the role of the 20th century, self-made American businesswoman. She had established herself as a pioneer of the modern black hair care and cosmetics industry, and set standards in the African-American community for corporate and community giving. An advisor to Presidents, Madam Walker was the first female African American millionaire in the United States that we have been able to document.

Tenacity and perseverance, faith in herself and in God, quality products, and "honest business dealings" were the elements and strategies she prescribed for aspiring entrepreneurs who requested the secret to her rags-to-riches ascent. "There is no royal flower strewn path to success," she once commented. "And if there is, I have not found it for if I have accomplished anything in life it is because I have been willing to work hard."

Recommended Activity: Try placing a pad and pencil next to your bed, and see what happens. Who knows what you might come up with in the middle of the night?

Chapter Twenty-One

Preparing for Graduation

Graduation is a ceremony to celebrate and recognize the successful completion of a particular course of study over a period of time. If you breezed through this book, over 20 minutes while living cross-country or waiting in an airport, then I would say that you have not completed this particular course of study. If, on the other hand, you have digested this book and taken notes, looked for new ideas, and have tried to get those ideas into the marketplace in whatever form possible, then you have indeed accomplished something important in the inventive process.

If you don't like to mark up your books, you might want to consider buying a good, used copy in which you are free to highlight, mark up and make notes. Our Idea Journal is being designed right now to take you day by day through the whole idea reception and development process, with the goal being for you to make notes and doodle ideas and potential.

Getting Started

This book has been designed to motivate you and stir up your creative gifts. If you feel more aware, educated, and motivated to develop your new' ideas as a result of your reading this far, then we have been successful. If you become rich and famous as a result, your family benefits, you are more fulfilled and productive, and society is blessed as a result, then I am satisfied.

Maybe your new idea has not hit yet. I said for years to a good friend of mine, "When you receive your new idea, please call me." When it hit in 1997, it was not long before I was on an airplane with an initial retainer check for the patent attorney. Two years later, we had a publicly traded company worth approximately $50-60 million.

You must do two things: (1) expect that powerful new idea to hit you––if not tomorrow, then this year, and if not this year, then next. I pray that it is so strong that it literally hits and stuns you with its power, intensity, and force; and (2) when it hits, reread this book from cover to cover. Go after it with everything you have. Develop it, live it, breathe it, just as I have done with this book manuscript.

As you head out into the real world to apply what you have learned, continue learning while you are doing. When you have successfully read, studied, perused and applied the lessons and wisdom of this book, we have a very attractive Certificate of Completion and Graduation as a gift for you to frame. This will remind you daily that you are an idea person and agent of change for the world.

Simply email me at mrd8542@aol.com and have the ISBN number of this book handy.

Let me leave you with one final thought: we began these studies with a quote from Proverbs 8:12: "I wisdom dwell with prudence, and find out knowledge of witty inventions." Wisdom has the ability to find out and distribute witty ideas and valuable inventions as she sees fit.

A man called Iames wrote the following:

> *If any of you lack wisdom, let him ask of God, that giveth to all men liberally, and upbraideth not; and it shall be given him. But let him ask in faith, nothing wavering. For he that wavereth is like a wave of the sea driven with the wind and tossed. Let the brother of low degree rejoice in that he is exalted:* (James 1:5-6, 9)

If you will ask God right now for the kind of wisdom that leads to valuable witty inventions, you can be confident that He will answer you in rich and surprising ways. Be ready for an adventure, and good luck!

Appendices

APPENDIX A
Typical Executive Summary

A typical executive summary is two-three pages in length and includes the following sections:

Introduction
Company Overview
Market Opportunity
Management
Breakthrough (or Disruptive) Technology
Market Approach and Business Strategy
Exit Strategy
© Copyright AtoZ International, Inc.
Date: Proprietary & Confidential

The following is a sample Executive Summary:

Executive Summary

Introduction
The Christian publishers located in the United States all face the same critical problem: how to locate promising authors and promote their books in a cost effective manner. It has been reported that publishers face severe shortages of blockbuster authors——proven performers

with Christian consumers who generate one or two new books each year.

The world's largest secular book publishers pay substantial advances to these major authors, including increasingly Christian writers, which makes it harder for the many smaller publishers to succeed and grow. Therefore, for this and other reasons, there is a significant consolidation going on in the publishing industry.

With the advent of Print-on-Demand book printing technology (POD using mainly IBM equipment), almost anyone can technically become a publisher. But, how to become a major publishing force, is the elusive question.

Company Overview

Spirit-Filled Books ("SFB" or the "Company"), an Oklahoma limited liability company, was formed as the final corporate structure to join forces to take advantage of a major vacuum and many available opportunities to publish and distribute mainly Christian books domestically and internationally. The three co-founders, with distinctive management strengths, all worked together for a major publishing and distributing house with strong authors and marketing channels.

It is estimated that the use of the Company's relationships, assets and strengths will significantly help the exploding Christian and secular publishing world meet the needs of many promising authors and expectant consumers and readers.

Market Opportunity

The Company's extensive research and efforts to date have resulted in seven current titles and five potential books and series each targeting a distinct large market segment, such as Charismatic financial and business subjects worldwide. These products and the market segments they target have tremendous upside potential. For example, the *God's Little Devotional* Series that one of the co-founders worked with, grew rapidly to become almost eighteen million dollars in annual revenue to its owners—almost 9,000,000 books sold to date. Another series routinely sold 500,000 per title; another recent hit sold thirteen million copies.

Just one series hit, like *God's Little Devotionals* (another great Tulsa-based success store: Honor Books) or *The Prayer of Jabez*, can make a great deal of money for its owners and investors that may result in an estimated Company valuation nearing $100 million.

Management

The management team of Spirit-Filled Books consists of individuals who collectively possess all the requisite skills to execute the Company's business plan:

- Nate Anderson
- Michael
- John
- Dr. John Avanzini, consulting author
- Michael Davis, financial consultant

Equally, members of the Advisory Board are all exceptionally well qualified to provide oversight and guidance during the Company's anticipated growth stages.

Breakthrough Strategy

The Company's existing authors have proprietary series planned, any one of which could catch fire and take off. Additionally, the principals have targeted major up and coming authors that could rival the success of writers like Joyce Meyer and the *Left Behind* series––not only within North America, but also worldwide.

In addition, the Company already has a very valuable list of churches and church bookstores that has proven extremely valuable to another Christian publisher. To add to that, there are many successful local and regional ministries that desire help in publishing and distributing their books and other printed materials.

The Project

TRP is producing a live theatrical concert based on Revelation, the last book of the Bible. This project is the logical extension of the vision for a solo presentation.

Appendix B
U.S. Angel Groups

1. Ad-Ventures, LLC

Ad-Ventures describes themselves as a launchpad for dynamic technology ventures like Internet startup iBoost.com or net veteran icom.com, in addition to being active in real estate developmcnt and entertainment ventures. Using a network of strategic partners. Ad-Ventures assists Internet and real-estate visionaries with the capital and strategic guidance needed to leap from napkin-penned ideas to global leadership. Ad-Ventures usually doesn't directly provide companies with money to grow their business, but rather works with Softbank.

2. AngelSociety

AngelSociety is a leading provider of information, communication, and transactional services for early stage private equity investors, early stage companies, and professional business service providers. Resources provided include Angel Advisor, an AngelSociety magazine from Bloomberg, AngelSociety Online, an Internet community, and AngelSociety Forums & Events, their conference and tradeshow business.

3. Angel Capital Electronic Network – ACE-Net

The Angel Capital Electronic Network called ACE-Net is a nationwide Internet based listing service that provides information to angel investors on small, dynamic, growing businesses seeking $250,000 – $5 million in equity financing. ACE-Net is sponsored by the office of Advocacy of the U.S. Small Business Administration and is a major effort to start systematizing and expanding information on firms seeking equity financing. The program was announced in 1996, and when it is fully operational it will be run as a private, independent, not for profit organization.

4. Angel Search

Angel Search at vfinance.com combs government records to gather investment data, industry preferences and total stock positions of America's wealthiest individuals. The site claims "Every individual in our database has a net worth of at least $1 million. AngelSearch™ is constantly updated, cleaned and checked for accuracy. You can search the database as many times as you like, result counts are always free. Once you get a count of wealthy individuals that match your needs, you can buy all matching records, a portion of the records, refine your search, or start a new one."

5. The Angels' Forum

The Angels' Forum is a group of private equity investors with diverse industry, gender, cultural, and business experience. The Angel Investors are united in their interest in investing both time and money in very early stage companies (typical investments would range from $50,000 – $500,000). Angels' Forum invests only in companies headquartered in the Greater San Francisco Bay Area.

6. Business Angels Pty. Ltd

Business Angels Pty. Ltd. is a central resource in Australia where both private investors and businesses register. The matching service's mission is to enable development of Australian technologies and small businesses (see articles below).

7. Business Partners

Business partners is a nationwide Internet-based service that connects Potential Partners, Angel Investors, Investment Bankers and Venture Capital firms. The Business Partners database allows interested parties to list under a topic of interest for free. Under each topic are SIC style categories, investment details, partnership criteria, location by state, city, and contact information. Members have Full access to the database of Potential Partners, Angel Investors, and Venture Capital opportunities.

8. The Capital Network

TCN is a non-profit, economic development organization created in response to a growing need to provide entrepreneurial ventures with training and access to investors. The Network offers investor-to-entrepreneur introduction services, educational programs, venture capital conferences, seminars, literature, software, and a network of experts and advisors.

9. Capitalyst, LLC

Formerly Amis Ventures, Capitalyst funds startup companies. Capitalyst addresses the private equity financing needs of entrepreneurs by providing an efficient early-stage funding process. In addition, Capitalyst enables qualified investors to locate, assess and co-invest in prescreened high potential startup opportunities with the Capitalyst affiliated StartUpFund One. Focused on the Northeast and Mid-Atlantic regions, Capitalyst is headquartered in Boston, Massachusetts, with a regional office in Washington, DC.

10. Connect Atlanta at Growco.com

Connect Atlanta provides a list that identifies local angel investor programs and seed capital investors.

11. Donmar Business Services

Donmarbiz' Angel Access facilitates communication among private investors and pre-screened, qualified entrepreneurial companies. The registry of Angel investors is based in New Jersey and continues expansion throughout the United States.

12. TheElevator

TheElevator's emphasis is in work germinating in the business schools, engineering programs, and entrepreneurial programs around major universities. Angels who are registered members of TheElevator browse hundreds of "elevator pitches" that have been classified according to: 1) type of business; 2) geographic location; 3) amount of money desired; and 4) experience of the entrepreneur.

13. garage.com

Garage.com provides entrepreneurs with assistance in obtaining seed level financing via mentoring and an investor network.

14. Gathering of Angels

The Gathering of Angels began in October, 1996 with the express purpose and mission to provide equity capital to the entrepreneurs of New Mexico. At that time, there were no Venture Capital firms represented in the state and the banks were generally not supportive of entrepreneurial ventures. Twenty-nine companies have received some level of funding, two firms have done up mergers into a public shell, and three have received venture capital funding.

15. International Capital Resources

International Capital Resources reports itself to be the oldest for-profit business introduction service in the U.S. and has developed a database of accredited business angel investors in North America. ICR otters Business Angel Financing Seminars several times during the year at different locations in the U.S.

16. New Vantage Group

New Vantage Group (NVG) manages early stage venture funds for active angel investors including the Dinner Club, LLC, The eMedia Club, LLC, and The Washington Dinner Club, LLC. NVG is also an advisor to WomenAngels.net. Sixty to eighty active angels have invested in each of these Funds, which co-invest with traditional venture capital funds. According to the Group, the Club/Fund concept has proven so successful in the Greater Washington area that NVG is now building a community of clubs nationally. In 2001, NVG is co-launching, with local managers, additional funds as part of the emerging NVG network of active angel venture funds.

17. The NYNMA Angel Investors Program

The NYNMA Angel Investors Program matches promising start-up companies with experienced Angel investors to facilitate the growth of New York's new media industry. According to the organization, about half of the companies that present at the monthly breakfast receive seed funding of up to $2,000,000. In order to receive funding, one of the company's executives must be a member of the New York New Media Association (NYNMA), companies should have their main office in the New York metropolitan area, and companies should be significantly involved in the new media industry.

18. Source Capital Network

The Source Capital Network is a members-only Internet site serving active angel investors for fast-growth venture opportunities. Entrepreneurs present their business plans to angel members using SCN's videos and audio format. Membership and presentation fees support the SourceCapital Network operation.

19. Venture Capital Money (VCmoney.com)

Venture Capital Money or VCmoney.com is a venture capital financing resource for entrepreneurs, providing sources and information on raising capital including Venture Capital financing and angel financing. For angels and investors, it provides information on joining or forming an angel group, and investment opportunities. Angel networks may also be interested in combining to form an SBIC. VCmoney.com also provides a Forum in which entrepreneurs, angels, and investors can share ideas, needs, and other information.

20. The Venture Site

The Venture Site uses the global scope of the World Wide Web to help and encourage commerce and industry in the United Kingdom. Specifically, The Venture Site provides Web-based advertising and matchmaking facilities for companies in search of venture capital and private investors.

21. Wellspring Angel Fund LLC

The Wellspring Angel Fund LLC is an early stage venture capital group composed of and run solely by angel investors, focusing on nurturing high-growth businesses that are developing innovative products and services in the information and electronic technology areas.

22. www.angelinvestors.org

www.angelinvestors.org is a non profit 501.c.6 corporation whose goal is to facilitate informed and profitable investments through an International League of Angels; empower Angels and Entrepreneurs through improved corporate governance, finance, and marketing; and strive to harmonize securities laws.

23. Venture Planning Associates

According to the firm, many of their projects are funded by angel sources, and often one investor will assist in the funding of multiple projects. The firm offers to teach you what you need to know to obtain angel investor funds. The firm also offers Private Equity funding reports, which provide "all information on the size and type of deal and the investors. All contact information, including phone and email is included. This firm showed $10.8 billion in investments in the second quarter of 2001."

24. Wye River Capital

Wye River Capital specializes in providing corporate finance, financial advisory, and merchant banking services to companies in the information, technology, and healthcare sectors. Wye River Capital's professionals have completed more than 200 equity, debt, and related transactions totaling over $15 billion during their collective careers. Based in Annapolis, Maryland, Wye River Capital will invest capital, raise funds through their network and provide other resources to help a company launch or build its business.

25. Youngentrepreneur.com

Youngentrepreneur.com features a Capital Search Engine billed as *the* place to look to find the funding your business needs.

Websites for Angel Groups

Go to *Inc. Magazine's* excellent web page, www.inc. com/search/2 3461.html, where they have lists of angel groups by region in the United States: National, Pacific Northwest, Southwest, Mid Atlantic, Northeast, North Central, California, South, and Midwest.

APPENDIX D

SCORE Association

"The SCORE Association, headquartered in Washington, D.C., is a nonprofit association dedicated to entrepreneurial education and the formation, growth and success of small businesses nationwide.

"SCORE'S 10,500 retired and working volunteers provide free business counseling and advice as a public service. SCORE is a resource partner with the U.S. Small Business Administration.

"SCORE offers

- Ask SCORE email advice online.
- Face-to-face business counseling at 389 chapters.
- Low-cost workshops at 389 chapters nationwide.
- Free and confidential small business counseling.

About SCORE's Services

"Working with our 389 local chapters, SCORE reaches small business owners across the country—from Maine to Hawaii. SCORE chapters serve as your local connection to small business know how.

"At SCORE, we realize that you have 1,001 tasks and one chance at business success. Establishing, growing, and improving a business takes a sophisticated mix of entrepreneurial vision, business management know how, and specialized knowledge. Through tree, small business counseling and support services, SCORE volunteers are here to keep your business going and growing.

"From marketing advice to finances, sales, and operations, SCORE counselors will help you find the answers. Just as important, counselors will help you develop and think through your business plan to make sure you're asking the right questions.

"When you seek help from a SCORE business counselor, you get the benefit of all his or her ideas—and the continuity of knowing that someone who knows and understands your small business is available for ongoing support. Seeking advice from a SCORE counselor provides a distinct advantage as you go forward."*—From SCORE'S website: www.score.org*

APPENDIX E

Links to Websites for Entrepreneurs

1) **U.S. Patent & Trademark Office** http://www.uspto.gov

2) **U.S. Copyright Office**: http://www.loc.gov/copyright/

3) **Christian Businessmen's Org.** http://www.cbmc.com/ "CBMC is Connecting Business Men to Christ, a worldwide network of business and professional men. Established in 1930 by a small group of businessmen, who shared the desire to communicate the eternal, life-saving message of Jesus Christ to others, CBMC continues to evangelize and disciple today's business and professional community."

4) **Full Gospel Businessmen's Org.** http://www.fgbmfi.org/ "The Full Gospel Business Men's Fellowship International is an organization sovereignly ordained by God...Today the Fellowship operates in 132 countries. Thousands of chapters hold meetings in small hamlets, farm towns, outlying suburbs and urban power centers. Breakfast, lunch and dinner, these meetings are a time of fellowship, outreach and personal ministry."

5) **Anointed for Business**

http://www.anointedforbusiness.org/

"Network with America's top Christian business leaders. Refresh, recharge and return to work with a new vision. The Anointed for Business Conference is a dynamic combination of business training, skill building, networking and spiritual refreshing that will take you and your company to a new level! You will enjoy powerful teaching, cutting-edge business training, anointed worship and will glean a harvest of breakthrough ideas and strategies."

6) **Gold Mine Development Company**

http://www.purposequest.com/

"Gold Mine Development Company (GMDC) takes its name from Dr. Stanko's first book. *Life is a Gold Mine: Can You Dig It?* GMDC's stated purpose is to help develop the gold in every individual. In 1985, Dr. Stanko began conducting seminars to help people become more productive and focused. The Life Is a Gold Mine seminar led to the book, and now Gold Mine Development Co. houses the worldwide efforts and resources of Dr. Stanko to continue to assist people as they search for purpose and meaning. His work has allowed him to assist companies and ministries become more focused as well."

APPENDIX F

Magazine Resources for Entrepreneurs

The Godly Business Woman's Magazine
"We believe that all women are business women so our magazine offers quality reading that allow women to grow and be informed as wives, mothers, singles, grandmothers and businesswomen. The only way to complete a task efficiently and completely is to have the tools for the trade. We want to offer you the tools for the trade."

Business Reform Magazine:
"Business Reform exists to assist Christian businesses and businesspeople in giving glory to God by applying the Word of the Lord to our work on earth."

Other helpful magazines:
Discovery, Entrepreneur, Fast Company, Forbes, Fortune Inc., Scientific American

APPENDIX G

Copyright Partner Nations

Listed Nations honor the Berne Convention; those with asterisks honor the UCC treaty:

Albania	Columbia	Guyana	Malta
Algeria	Congo	Haiti	Mauritania
Andorra*	Costa Rica	Honduras	Mauritius
Argentina	Cote d'Ivoire	Hungary	Mexico
Australia	Croatia	Iceland	Moldova
Austria	Cuba	India	Monaco
Azerbaijan*	Cyprus	Indonesia	Mongolia
Bahamas	Czech Rep.	Ireland	Morocco
Bahrain	Congo	Israel	Namibia
Bangladesh	Denmark	Italy	Netherlands
Barbados	Dom. Rep.	Jamaica	New Zealand
Belarus	Ecuador	Japan	Nicaragua
Belgium	Egypt	Kazakhstan	Niger
Belize*	El Salvador	Kenya	Nigeria
Benin	Equ. Guinea	Rep. of Korea	Norway
Bolivia	Estonia	Laos*	Pakistan
Bosnia	Fiji	Latvia	Panama
Botswana	Finland	Lebanon	Paraguay
Brazil	France	Lesotho	Peru
Bulgaria	Gabon	Liberia	Philippines
Burkina Faso	Gambia, The	Libya	Poland
Cambodia*	Georgia	Liechtenstein	Portugal

Cameroon	Germany	Lithuania	Romania
Canada	Ghana	Luxembourg	Russian Fed.
Cape Verde	Greece	Macedonia	Rwanda
C. African Rep	Grenada	Madagascar	St. Cristopher
Chad	Guatemala	Malawi	Nevis
Chile	Guinea	Malaysia	Saint Lucia
China	Guinea-Bissau	Mali	Saint Vincent
Saudi Arabia*	Senegal	Singapore	Slovakia
Slovenia	South Africa	Spain	Sri Lanka
Suriname	Swaziland	Sweden	Switzerland
Tajikistan*	Tanzania	Thailand	Togo
Trinidad	Tobago	Tunisia	Turkey
Ukraine	U.K.	Uruguay	Vatican City
Venezuela	Yugoslavia	Zambia	Zimbabwe

APPENDIX H

Just for Authors

1. **What is an ISBN number?**

The ISBN system stands for International Standard Book Number system, which uniquely identifies all books published worldwide. These have become a very useful standard for all aspects of the book business including ordering, accounting, and inventory control. About one million ISBN's are assigned each year for English-language publications alone.

Each ISBN is a unique number, identifying one title by type of binding or edition or publisher. So, for example, the same basic book published by different publishers over time in various hardback and paperback versions and different editions, could have a number of different ISBN's to keep track of the various combinations.

The first six digits identity the particular publisher, for example 1-56731, which is MJF Books, Fine Communications, NYC. The next three digits, 349 in this example, uniquely identifies the title *Personal Best* (by Joe Tye) within one of the blocks of ISBN's allotted to MJF Books (publishers buy these numbers in blocks because they are much cheaper that way: a block of ten costs about $220.) The final digit is a mathematical check digit. These numbers are kept current in a worldwide database so that bookstores and librarians can easily determine where to purchase a copy.

2. **What is a barcode?**

Barcode scanners are now used everywhere at retail checkout counters. At bookstores, in particular, there is a special type of barcode which complies with the Bookland EAN/ISBN standard (different than the UPC standard for other types of retail products). If you plan on selling your books through retail channels, this barcode will be needed.

Most of the book barcodes that I have examined follow the format of 9 78xxx xxxxx9 – where the x's are the ISBN less the last cheek digit. The optional last digits (90000>) on the right side are the fixed retail price in one currency. 90000 happens to mean that the retail price was unknown at the time of issuance.

United States publishers may obtain ISBN numbers from the ISBN Agency R.R. Bowker, 121 Chanlon Road, New Providence, NJ 07974. Phone toll-free 1-888/269-5372. Fax 1-908/665-3502.

3. **Tell me again about the copyright notice, and depositing two copies with the National Library:**

First of all, try not to freely circulate your materials without a copyright notice because that behavior can be generally regarded as saving to the world, "This material is now in the public domain." Therefore, include within your manuscript and book the statement: "© copyright 2002 by J. Franklin Smith" – ideally on the reverse side of the title page. You may want to expand this with another statement like: "All rights reserved. No part of this publication may be reproduced, stored in a retrieval system, or transmitted, in any form or by any means, electronic, mechanical, photocopying, recording, or otherwise, without the written prior permission of the author. Contact the author at..." or "in care of the publisher."

In the United States, you then should deposit two copies of your book with the library of Congress. In Canada, with the National Library. This helps with library orders and copyright disputes.

ABOUT THE AUTHOR

MICHAEL R. DAVIS is an independent financial strategist assisting new companies during their start up stage. He is currently serving as a director of Oryxe Energy Int. Inc., an innovative fuel additive company. Michael graduated from Harvard College and pursued graduate studies at the Harvard Business School.

He is the author of *The Secret of FirstFruits* and *Witty Inventions*. He also publishes a weekly e-column called Reflections™ for Christian entrepreneurs and marketplace leaders around the world.

Has God given you a marvelous idea? Here's how to profitably develop it -

If you've been entrusted with a great idea from God, b??? develop it, finance it, protect it, and market it. *The Chr???* is just the book you need! Harvard graduate and former student of Dr. Peter Drucker, Mike Davis has helped many creative people move from the early stages of the drawing board to the financial success of the boardroom.

In these pages you'll learn:

* How to evaluate whether your ideas have commercial potential
* Where to get financing for your God-given project
* How to protect your creative ideas from unscrupulous thieves
* Step-by-step instructions to help take your new product to market
* Ideas to help you promote & market your product or service
  ——and much more!

"Many people need help in understanding how to make business ideas a reality. Mike Davis is superb at doing just that. If you're tired of talking about your ideas and not seeing them come to pass, this book is for you!"

——Dr. John W. Stanko,
founder, PurposeQuest International

"Michael Davis has continued to recognize that...our loving Father is more than willing to reveal to us the strategies aid knowledge that we need to walk in the creative destiny He has for each one of us."

—*Richard & Mary Morris,*
Mary Germain International Ministries

"It will be a great help for people who have ideas but don't know what to do about them."

—*Mrs. Evelyn (Oral) Roberts*

EPILOGUE (Updated) and PRAYER

1. You're going to want to have a good website with email capabilities (like, "info@abcwebsite.com)

Credibility

One of the main reasons you should have a website for your business is to increase your organization's credibility. Chances are there are several providers offering a similar service to yours. One way you can stand out is by having a website that looks good and clearly communicates quality information to your consumers.

Without a website, people may question your legitimacy as a business. Having a website is an opportunity to make a great first impression and give people comfort that you're a real business.[12]

2. You're going to want to hire a good securities attorney as fundraising counsel. Consider reading *Capital for Keeps*, Russell Weigel III author, foreword by former SEC Commissioner. Mistakes here can land you in jail

3. You're going to want to do favors for others, especially those who cannot repay you. Have a specific cause and purpose to support with your revenues and profits, like Tom's™ and 'Lil Bubbies™

4. If you're spiritually-minded, you're going to want to find a good business apostle, accurate prophets and powerful intercessors to help guide and support you: those opposing you are not only visible, but also invisible

5. Finally, you are not reading this book by accident nor chance: ask Your Higher Power to reveal itself to you, do it now quietly in the privacy of your mind. See what happens.

---

[1] Forbes, Why Every Business Needs A Website (forbes.com)
[2] Some contract their website construction in India; also, GoDaddy now offers Airo™ using Artificial Intelligence (AI) to build it automatically for you to easily get started

That they also will build great businesses and help others in need;
For Your purposes I pray,
Amen."

We've sowed this book into your life, career and business; please consider gifting a copy to someone else.

Prayer of impartation

Please let me pray for you now –

"Father, Who made all things, I pray now for this reader
that they come to know you personally and
That they will find Your track for them to run on
For wisdom and strength and favor
For ideas, strategies and good partners
For integrity and righteousness
That they also will build great businesses and help others
in need;
For Your purposes I pray,
Amen."

Printed in the United States
by Baker & Taylor Publisher Services